RENO

HUB OF THE WASHOE COUNTRY

Engine No. 1, a horse-drawn steam water pumper, was captured in this circa 1905 photograph in front of the Reno firehouse. Weighing approximately 9,400 pounds, this equipment was used to fight fires as early as the 1880s. Courtesy, Nevada Historical Society

R E N O

HUB OF THE WASHOE COUNTRY
AN ILLUSTRATED HISTORY
BY WILLIAM D. ROWLEY

"PARTNERS IN PROGRESS"
BY ROBERT NYLEN

INTRODUCTION
BY PHILLIP I. EARL

Produced in Cooperation with the
University of Nevada Reno

Windsor Publications, Inc.
Woodland Hills, California

Windsor Publications, Inc.
History Books Division
Publisher: John M. Phillips
Editorial Director: Lissa Sanders
Production Supervisor: Katherine Cooper
Senior Picture Editor: Teri Davis Greenberg
Senior Corporate History Editor: Karen Story
Corporate History Editor: Phyllis Gray
Marketing Director: Ellen Kettenbeil
Production Manager: James Burke
Design Director: Alexander D'Anca
Art Production Manager: Dee Cooper
Typesetting Manager: E. Beryl Myers
Proofreading Manager: Doris R. Malkin

Windsor Publications' Staff for
  Reno: Hub of the Washoe Country
Editor: Pamela Taylor
Text Editor: Lissa Sanders
Picture Editor: Susan Wells
Sales Manager: Steve Allison
Sales Representative: Robert Fay
Editorial Assistants: Susan Block, Patricia Buzard,
  Patricia Dailey, Judy Hunter
Compositors: Barbara Neiman, Cynthia Pinter
Proofreaders: Lynn Johnson, Jeff Leckrone
Production Artists: Beth Bowman, Ellen Hazeltine
Layout Artists: Ellen Hazeltine, Melinda Wade

Library of Congress Cataloguing in Publication Data
Rowley, William D.
  Reno: hub of the Washoe country.
  " 'Partners in progress' by Robert Nylen'': p. 96
  Bibliography: p. 123
  Includes index.
  1. Reno (Nev.) — History. 2. Washoe Country (Nev.) —
History. 3. Reno (Nev.) — Description. 4. Reno (Nev.) —
Industries. I. University of Nevada, Reno. II. Title.
F849.R4R69 1984   979.3'55   83-23422

ISBN 0-89781-080-5

CONTENTS

ACKNOWLEDGMENTS

The writing of this short history of Reno has been designed to offer a broad thematic approach to the history of the city within the context of national history. Emphasis has been placed upon the general picture rather than upon the sea of detail so common in local histories. Sometimes it is more important to see the forest rather than dwell upon an individual tree. Still some timber stands so tall that it must be recognized and analyzed in relation to the times under consideration. At this point the roles of various personalities emerge in the life of a community. Many of these "tall timbers" appear in these pages such as Francis G. Newlands, George Wingfield, Pat McCarran, E.E. Roberts, Anne Martin, and Earl Wooster to name but a few.

Support and help from people in Reno's and Nevada's historical community played a large role in the making of this book. In the Special Collections Room of Getchell Library on the campus of the University of Nevada-Reno, Ellen Guerricagoitia, Tim Gorelangton, and Lee Kosso cheerfully accepted endless questions and requested searches. At the Nevada Historical Society, Director Peter Bandurraga, Eslie Cann, Phillip I. Earl, Lee Mortensen, and Robert Nylen were valuable allies in bringing forth secrets from the archives. Conversations with Guy Louis Rocha, Head of Nevada State Archives, helped shaped questions important to the study. My colleagues in UNR's Department of History, Jerome E. Edwards, Russell R. Elliott, Wilbur S. Shepperson, and Michael J. Brodhead, read and criticized materials with an oftentimes uncomfortable frankness. Kathryn M. Totton of the Government Publications Department in the Getchell Library helped assemble important statistics from that complicated domain. To my wife, Patricia Rowley, I wish to acknowledge assistance in picture research and caption writing. Of course, shortcomings in the text are my responsibility.

It is the author's hope that *Reno: Hub of the Washoe Country* will offer further insight into our ever unfolding attempts to make sense out of our past and give identities to our present and future.

WILLIAM D. ROWLEY

INTRODUCTION

Just as ancient civilizations and nonliterate peoples are best understood through the study of their artifactual remains, so it is that visual images—photographs—provide a window on the past that eludes conventional historical studies. Not that this history of Reno is only a "picture book." It is not. In addition to making use of photographs from libraries, museums, and treasured private collections, Professor Rowley places Reno in the context of its times and documents the complex interplay of social, economic, and political forces which have sustained the growth and development of the community since its founding in 1868.

Most American cities began as regional marketing centers which developed into metropolitan complexes serving a broader outlying area, but Reno came into being as a railroad town, a fact that those of us who are periodically held up at Southern Pacific grade crossings are not likely to forget anytime soon. What Reno has become is the substance of its history—a railhead for the cattle community, a force to be reckoned with in the political life of the state, a mecca for divorce-seekers and, in recent years, a destination for those Americans seeking to "sin a little" at the luxurious casinos which have become a part of life in Reno.

Professor Rowley's history of Reno is not merely a sifting through facts, but an attempt to evaluate and understand their meaning in light of the changing character of the American West, regional and national economic priorities, and the vagaries of moral precepts which have swept the land over the years. Writing of the history of Reno in such broad terms does not exclude considerations of all that makes Reno unique, however—the persistently high crime rate, the rather odd brand of morality which exists alongside legalized gambling, the Old West themes embodied in the annual Reno Rodeo, the many parks, the beauty of the Truckee River, the love of Reno's old-timers for this "City of Trembling Leaves," as one famous novelist described the city. Considerable attention is also given to the manner in which the citizens of Reno have viewed their future and that of their community and what this means for the future itself. The book also includes concise histories of many of the principal business concerns which have contributed to the growth and prosperity of Reno. In sponsoring this publication, the University of Nevada adds another dimension to its efforts to serve the people of Nevada and preserve the rich heritage of the community where the school has been located for nearly a century.

PHILLIP I. EARL
CURATOR OF EXHIBITS
NEVADA HISTORICAL SOCIETY

CHAPTER ONE

THE RUSH TO WASHOE

Western Nevada is one of those remarkable places in the American West that blends a crisp sunlit climate with spectacular mountain and desert scenery. Surrounded by desert and wooded mountain ranges, the glittering lights of Reno command the night sky over the Truckee Meadows. Through the years this once small town emerged as the transportation and commercial center for a mining and ranching country. The growth of gaming enterprises since the 1930s crowned Reno's preeminence as the urban center of northwestern Nevada.

The boundaries of this region are marked by the forested high Sierra in the west and a mountainous, endless gray-sage desert to the east. Lying on the edge of the intermountain area known as the Great Basin, the region's major rivers drain toward the interior and not the sea. Reno shares the mountain valleys of western Nevada with its sister city of Sparks, the state capital at Carson City, and the communities of Minden and Gardnerville. The aging remnant of the once-great Queen of the Comstock, Virginia City, looks down from its decaying past upon the valleys that harbor the cities of the 20th century. Above the valleys of this land, Lake Tahoe's cold, blue waters provide refuge from summer heat, as they have done since humans first came to this place. All of these communities, including the "lake of the sky," are nestled in the Washoe Country. (Only the southern edge of the modern Washoe *County*, however, touches this ancient land.)

The name given to this part of Nevada comes from the original Washoe or Washo Indian inhabitants (early visitors tended to spell the name "Wassau") who lived in a migratory pattern between the desert valleys in winter and the high Sierra mountain lakes and meadows during the summer.

The lands of western Nevada were not wholly the province of the small Washoe tribe. The Northern Paiutes, far more numerous and even warlike, centered their existence around a great desert lake later called Pyramid Lake by the explorer John C. Frémont. The Paiutes feasted in the spring upon the spawning run of the cutthroat trout from the lake, and dispersed during the summer in small bands, gathering the food from the deserts to the south and the east. Many assembled again in the fall to harvest the pine nuts from the single-leaf piñon pine trees in the Virginia range, where the Comstock Lode was eventually discovered. The pine nut was an important staple that could be stored through winter, protecting the Paiutes against the "starving time" in the early spring before winter broke its grip on the eastern slopes of the Sierra and the surrounding cold desert.

The people of these mountains and sage deserts were survivors in every respect of the word, utilizing almost every possible food resource in their sparse environment. Among these foods were the roots of marshland plants. Cattail roots were roasted before eating; cane plants were split open and dried in the sun and the pulpy insides scraped out and pressed together. From Great Basin wild rye, wild rice, and bunch grass, seeds were harvested then ground into a meal with wild sunflower seeds and baked into cakes. Fly larvae gathered from the shores of the Humboldt and Carson rivers were rolled together into balls for winter storage. Grasshoppers and crickets pounded into a mash and mixed with animal grease made a nutritious chocolate-colored compound. Rabbits were among the small animals which added variety to the diet. In ritualized rabbit drives the hunters chased them into entangling nets where they were stomped and clubbed. White sage provided a medicinal tea during some of the long, hard, cold winters. Antelope and deer occasionally were brought down with primitive weapons but their role in the diet was limited. Clearly this was a society that rarely knew abundance. In the desert the small bands of people (20 to 25) kept in constant movement in search of food as they followed the practices of a typical hunter-gatherer culture. Still, the life of the Great Basin Indian knew festivals, the richness of the fish harvest at Pyramid Lake, and the social pleasures of the pine-nut gathering each fall.

This version of the rush to Washoe appeared in J. Ross Brown's
Crusoe's Island: Sketches of Adventure in California and Washoe
in 1867.

Captain John C. Frémont, a legendary Western explorer, conducted an expedition into Nevada in 1844. From Cirker, Dictionary of American Portraits, *Dover, 1967*

An experienced mountain man, Joseph Reddeford Walker led an expedition down the Humboldt and across Nevada in 1833. Courtesy, Nevada Historical Society

Trapper Peter Skene Ogden traveled the length of the Great Basin to the Gulf of California by 1830. From Cirker, Dictionary of American Portraits, *Dover, 1967*

Contact between the Euro-Americans and the Native Americans of western Nevada began in the early fur-trade explorations in the 1820s and continued through the army-sponsored expeditions of John C. Frémont in the 1840s. The explorers who came in that period saw the Indians of the Great Basin as little more than a part of the indigenous animal life. Fur trapper-explorer Jedediah Smith was one of the first whites to record what he considered the unfortunate condition of the natives. He wrote of "those children of nature... unintelligent kind of beings" and asserted, "They form a connecting link between the animal and intellectual creation and quite in keeping with the country in which they are located."

Sources about Native American impressions of the white men are often obscured by time and the absence of written records. Many times the imagination of the historical novelist can best capture some of the lost events and meanings of a people's life. The novel *Rabbit Boss* (1974) by Thomas Sanchez is a fascinating attempt to describe how the Washoes may have lived, thought, and felt, beginning with a scene in which several Indians watch, horrified, the cannibalism of the Donner party under the privation of winter snows.

The fur-trade expeditions provided much of the early geographical knowledge about the intermountain region. The Joseph Walker expedition across the Great Basin from the Salt Lake area in 1833 followed the course of a river with great importance in Washoe Country history, the Humboldt. The expedition followed the course of the Humboldt, or "Barren" River, as they termed it, until it disappeared into the desert in a series of sinks in the Big Meadows near present-day Lovelock. Then they struck out across the 40-mile desert to reach another river which would eventually be called the Carson. One member of the party wrote of this land: "Everything here seems to declare that, here man shall not dwell." (Earlier, the Canadian fur trapper from the Hudson's Bay Company, Peter Skene Ogden, had already discovered the "Barren" River, which he dubbed the "Unknown" River.) By 1830 he traversed the entire length of the Great Basin from north to south along the eastern slopes of the Sierra all the way to the Gulf of California.

This small, unimpressive river in north-central Nevada guided travelers (first exploratory parties, then California-bound settlers) across the desert toward California. Unfortunately for the emigrants, the river ended and the desert began 40 miles short of the Sierra slope. This was the final barrier to California. After the ordeal of the desert, which was a test of courage and endurance for man and animal alike, the travelers sought the waters of either the Truckee or the Carson river which could offer relief from the alkali sands.

The Bidwell-Bartleson party in 1841 became the first California emigrants to pass through western Nevada's Washoe Country. They made it, after much tribulation, but one of the leaders, Bartleson, vowed that he detested the country and would return to his home in Missouri as soon as possible. To early travelers the only offerings of western Nevada were its flowing rivers and restful meadows before the challenge of the mountain passes.

In 1843 Joseph B. Chiles and the mountain man-turned-trail-guide Joseph Walker brought an emigrant party over the Humboldt Trail and into western Nevada before they left southward to cross the mountains over Walker Pass. In the following year, 1844—the same year that Frémont came into western Nevada—the Elisha Stevens party moved out from

Below: This sketch of the "pyramid" was redrawn from the original in Frémont's 1845 report. Charles Preuss, Frémont's assistant in topography, was the original artist. The party saw the lake January 10, 1844, and named the desert lake Pyramid four days later. Courtesy, Nevada Historical Society

the sinks of the Humboldt. There they had made the decision to go west instead of south toward the Carson River. An Indian made markings in the sand for them indicating a river and a possible pass over the mountains to the west. His name sounded something like "Truckee." When the emigrants finally reached the river, they expressed their pleasure with the refreshing stream by naming it in honor of the Paiute who befriended them. From the Truckee Meadows they followed the stream up into the mountains. The Stevens party became the first to open the Truckee Pass across the Sierra that would be known after the Donner tragedy in the winter of 1846-1847 as Donner Pass.

When army explorer John C. Frémont first entered what was to become western Nevada, he came down from the Oregon country on the east side of the Cascades and Sierra. He plodded through the inhospitable deserts to the north until he was finally rewarded for his laborious trek by the discovery of a great desert lake in January of 1844. He named it Pyramid because he believed that an island in the lake resembled the pyramids of Egypt. Frémont's first impression of the

lake, so his journals tell us, was a "sheet of green water, some 20 miles broad." The lake provided welcome relief to Frémont's party of 40 men who were burdened with a French-made howitzer which would later be abandoned in the Sierra.

On the southern end of the lake, Frémont met the Paiutes, who, he reported, lived prosperously on the abundant lake fish. After many weeks in the northern deserts, the exploring party eagerly traded articles for the lake's delicious trout. While the Paiutes were the first tribe of this western Nevada country encountered by Frémont, he saw signs of others: smoke signals from the nearby mountains announced his arrival as he moved farther south into the Truckee Meadows and the Carson Valley. In addition he saw the fish weirs of the Washoes in the streams running down the Sierra. As he crossed the Sierra somewhere in the vicinity of Carson Pass during February 1844, he caught sight of the blue waters of Lake Tahoe in the distance. The next year once again found Frémont traveling through Nevada toward California. This time he named the Humboldt River, *Walker* River, and *Wal-*

ker Lake, as he had named Carson River and Carson Lake the year before. His name for the Truckee, "The Salmon Trout River," did not remain. For Nevada, Frémont was chiefly a name-giver. His other contribution was that his party demonstrated scientifically that this was an area of interior drainage.

By the mid-1840s Nevada and its western portion served merely as a land bridge to a winterless place of fertile valleys owned by Mexico and called California. But in this decade occurred many events that would change the history of the Far West.

Bernard DeVoto, in his award-winning *1846: Year of Decision* describes four decisions in that crucial year that affected the American West. They were: the war with Mexico that resulted in the American acquisition of the Southwest; Brigham Young's decision to move the persecuted Mormons to the base of the Wasatch Mountains near the Great Salt Lake; the Donner party's decision to take the Hastings Cutoff south of the Oregon Trail (delaying their crossing of the Sierra until the winter storms struck); and the Oregon boundary settlement with Great Britain.

The first three of these decisions helped shape the future of western Nevada. The first made the intermountain region a part of the United States; the second brought a population of religious refugees to the eastern half of the Great Basin (some of these would eventually make settlements in the western portion of the Basin). The tragedy of the Donner party linked forever the Truckee River Pass route through the Sierra with feelings of horror and foreboding.

The year 1848 also had momentous consequences for the western Great Basin. In that year gold was discovered on one of the branches of the American River in California. By the end of the year President James K. Polk had the pleasure of announcing to Congress and the nation that Providence had blessed the newly acquired territories and the nation with fabulous gold discoveries in the streams of the Sierra. Throughout the Mississippi Valley and the East Coast feverish preparations began during the winter 1848-1849 for the rush to California. A majority came by sea around Cape Horn or over the Isthmus of Panama, but thousands came overland; walking or riding the trails to California. One wayfarer bound for the goldfields, Alfred Doten, boarded ship in Plymouth, Massachusetts in March of 1849 and made it to San Francisco by November. Doten eventually came to Nevada in 1863 and became a reporter for the *Gold Hill News* on the Comstock. He kept a remarkably descriptive diary of his life in Nevada, now a principal source for the period, until his death in 1903.

Those who came overland traveled for the most part over the California Trail—along the Humboldt and then across western Nevada crossing either over the Truckee/Donner Pass or pushing on to the Carson River to a place called Ragtown, and then south and west over the Carson Pass to Placerville (then called Hangtown), the gateway to the rich motherlode country. One historian of the California Trail estimates that 22,500 people followed it overland in 1849; 45,000 in 1850; only perhaps 5,000 in 1851; then up to nearly 52,000 in 1852.

By 1849 California, with its suddenly large population, wrote a state constitution and requested statehood from Congress. The quick rise of California to statehood underlined the dilemma Congress faced in bringing civil government to the newly acquired Southwest after the Treaty of Guadalupe Hidalgo ended the Mexican War in 1848. California's demand for statehood pushed Congress into action with passage of the Compromise of 1850 that included the admission of California as a free state.

Important for the future of Nevada, the Compromise created the Territory of Utah that extended from the Rocky Mountains to the eastern boundary of California. This western portion of the Great Basin was placed by Congress under Mormon government in Salt Lake City; while religious leader Brigham Young was made governor of the new territory. It was extensive, but destined to be reduced by the creation of the Nevada Territory in 1861. A quick glance at a population map from the Rockies to California in 1850 reveals a religious population to the east living in the Latter-day Saints' temple city of Salt Lake. Across the Great Basin and over the mountains a rowdy, transient mining population thrived in a land of Eden called California. The land between California and Salt Lake City was a virtual Land of Nod—east of Eden and west of "Zion"'s religious settlements. It was held in low regard as a place for serious settlement, even unfit for habitation, possibly a place of exile.

But shrewd Mormon businessmen in 1850 saw the possibility of a lucrative trade with the overland migration at the base of the Sierra in western Utah Territory. That year brought Joseph DeMont and his clerk, Hampton S. Beatie, to the Carson River Valley near the Sierra where they traded with the overland migration to the goldfields until the end of the season. Before winter set in, most of the party headed back to Salt Lake City. It had been an eventful summer in western Utah. Not only were these ambitious traders present, but one of the California-bound gold parties found placer gold in the streams along the side of Six Mile Canyon that reached up from the overland trail as it stretched along the Carson River. This was in a ravine that led up toward the mountain that harbored the rich and undiscovered Comstock

Mormon businessman John Reese founded Mormon Station in June 1851. Located in Carson Valley, Mormon Station was the first permanent settlement in what is today Nevada. At that time it was located at the western edge of the Utah Territory. Courtesy, Nevada Historical Society

Brigham Young served as governor of the Utah Territory from 1850 to 1857. From Cirker, Dictionary of American Portraits, *Dover, 1967*

Lode.

News of a limited gold strike and reports of a profitable summer's trade, as well as the beautiful setting of the Carson Valley, brought the Mormon businessman John Reese to Carson Valley in 1851. He and his companions were not Mormon missionaries, but straightforward businessmen bent on offering a service and earning a profit in trade, and possibly in mining. At a point south on the Carson River and against the steep rise of the Sierra, Reese's party constructed the first permanent white settlement in the future state and territory of Nevada. It was known as Mormon Station and became the focal point of activities in western Utah Territory. With this permanent trading station at hand, additional traders, miners, and farmer-ranchers started appearing. Their settlements reached from the Honey Lake agricultural area (present day Susanville, California) in the north to the rich valleys around the forks of the Carson River in the south.

Inevitably tensions followed between the Mormon-dominated local government and the non-Mormons outside of the favored circle. Petitions to the California legislature urged an extension of its laws across the mountains to free the area from the rule of those who were looked upon with suspicion because of their practice of polygamy. By 1855 Mor-

monism underwent a revival and regeneration of the faith that drew Brigham Young's attention to securing a stronger hold on neglected western Utah—a hold that was being threatened by protests and petitions against Utah's authority over the western counties.

The church decided to call Orson Hyde, one of the Council of Twelve, to lead a Mormon migration to the valleys of western Utah. Hundreds of the faithful began arriving and settled in the valleys, including beautiful Washoe Valley, 30 miles north of Mormon Station. Hyde became chief probate judge, renamed Mormon Station Genoa (after Columbus' birthplace), and founded Franktown in the Washoe Valley. He hoped Franktown would be the center of a Mormon population on this side of the Great Basin as Salt Lake City was the center on the other side. These hard-working farmers inspired by a religious zeal diligently plowed the lands leading up from Washoe Lake, installed crude irrigation systems, and began their housing utilizing boards milled by water power gushing from the Sierra behind the settlements.

All of this promising enterprise was interrupted in the summer of 1857 when the call came from Brigham Young that all of the faithful should return to Salt Lake City for the defense of "Zion." The occasion was the so-called Mormon War of

that year which saw federal troops advancing over the plains to Salt Lake to remove Young as territorial governor and ensure the enforcement of federal law in the territory. Those who departed left the fruits of two years of work behind them. The offer of protection by the Gentile community was offered to any reluctant to return, but few accepted.

The much-feared confrontation in Utah never took place. A compromise between the Mormon hierarchy in the territory and federal troops was negotiated. It saw the removal of Young as governor and the peaceful passage of the troops through the city. The greatest impact that the war had on the western counties was the removal of an influential population and the creation of a governmental vacuum. The remaining populace formed provisional governments in 1857 and 1859. The latter was headed by Isaac Roop from the Honey Lake settlements. Petitions flowed forth to Washington from this makeshift government for a separate territorial status.

After the excitement of Mormon industry in the valleys, a profound stillness prevailed. Miners probed up Gold and Six Mile canyons toward Sun Mountain (Mount Davidson) where the Comstock Lode would be discovered in 1859. Already two brothers from Pennsylvania, Ethan and Hosea Grosh, were making significant discoveries and crudely assaying ore in their prospector's hut. A series of misfortunes, however,

resulting in their untimely deaths prevented the world from knowing about their fabulous discovery of silver and gold ore in the mountain.

It fell to a group of unnotable souls to come upon rich outcroppings of ore on the face of the mountain. In January 1859 James Finney and others struck into the famous lode in the Gold Hill area of the Comstock. On the other end of the lode at the beginning of Six Mile Canyon, Patrick McLaughlin and Peter O'Riley made a similar discovery in June 1859. Then along came Henry P. Comstock, who demanded a share claiming part ownership in the spring surrounding the outcropping. His boisterous personality and loud-mouthed bragging about "his discovery" caused the miners to unwittingly refer to the entire ledge as the Comstock Lode. In a similar manner, the largest town on the Comstock obtained its name of Virginia City from James Finney: his nickname, "Old Virginny," stemmed from his birthplace in the Old Dominion.

Careful assays in Nevada City and Grass Valley, California in June of 1859 confirmed that fantastic gold and silver discoveries had been made in the Washoe Country across the mountains. Preliminary findings showed that the ore assayed out at $876 in gold per ton and an unbelievable $3,000 per ton in silver ($300 per ton for gold was considered a good paying claim at the time).

Throughout the California gold country the cry of "silver and gold across the mountains" was heard. In the summer of 1859 and through the winter of 1859-1860, the "Rush to

Chief Winnemucca, or Poito, was the leader of the Pyramid Lake Paiutes during the deadly winter of 1859-1860. His son Numaga, the Paiute war chief, led the attack that defeated Major William M. Ormsby and his troops. From History of Nevada, *Thompson and West, 1881*

Washoe" was on. Up to 6,000 miners, teamsters, tradesmen, merchants, and camp followers made their way over the mountains. The influx of people caused problems. The first and most obvious was the absence of effective civil government. Ever since the withdrawal of the Mormons, local government had been conspicuously absent in western Utah Territory. Little interest was shown in the provisional government of Isaac Roop after the excitement on the Comstock began. The territorial government in Utah stood helpless to exert its authority in the face of the arrival of a fast-living, rambunctious mining population.

San Francisco newspapers were fearful about the chances of maintaining the peace in the Washoe Country. In February 1860, the *San Francisco Bulletin* declared:

There is no government. Nominally the Mormon government bears sway over that portion of the territory as well as over Salt Lake City. But practically Mormon laws are a nullity, they are not enforced, nor could they be . . . . It is to be hoped that congress will give this matter an early consideration and save the people from those scenes of lawless violence, which all men fear, but which cannot be averted, except by such action as the government at Washington may take on their behalf.

The winter 1859-1860 not only saw the arrival of rowdy miners, but also cold and snow that persisted into the springtime months as winter so often does in this country. The Rush to Washoe by so many white people did not escape the notice of the Pyramid Lake Paiutes, who were themselves suffering with the extended winter. Unrest grew among the tribesmen because of disputes and mistreatment at the hands of the ever-growing white population. The older chiefs tried to check the discontent and threats of reprisals. Suddenly an incident ignited the tempers beyond control. Two young Indian women had been abducted and taken to a trading post on the lower Carson River. The result was predictable. An attack upon and burning of the Williams' Trading Station followed with three white men dying at the hands of Indians.

Throughout the valleys and mountains the fear of Indian war spread as rapidly as news of the fabulous Comstock discoveries. From the Carson City area and the Comstock, Major William M. Ormsby gathered 105 volunteers. They intended to march against Pyramid Lake on a punitive expedition. What ensued was a colossal disaster for Ormsby and the volunteers. As they moved down the Truckee toward the lake, the white men were waylaid by a superior Paiute force under the leadership of war chief Numaga, son of the old Chief Winnemucca. Ormsby died on the field of battle along with 75 of his men. The defeat was thorough and demoralizing, and now fear of the aggressive Paiutes alarmed even the governor of California. Virginia City prepared for an invasion and isolated ranchers fled to towns and forts.

After the debacle on May 12, 1860, another army

15

Myron C. Lake settled in the Truckee Meadows in 1861, taking over a previous way station that he soon built into Lake's Crossing. Courtesy, Nevada Historical Society

Charles Crocker, Central Pacific Railroad official, negotiated a depot and townsite location in the Truckee Meadows with Myron C. Lake in 1868. Courtesy, Nevada Historical Society

including 549 volunteers and 207 regular army took to the field. This time more caution was exercised in approaching the lake. On May 31 the Paiutes met the force head on but were dispersed with heavy losses and forced to retreat. They hurriedly left their settlements at Pyramid and fled into the trackless deserts to the north. After destroying the Indians' shelters and food supplies, the volunteers returned to the Comstock and their towns in California while the regular army pursued the tribe in hopes of bringing it to peace terms. By the end of summer, peace was restored and the army moved to the new Fort Churchill constructed on the nearby lower reaches of the Carson River. The tribe was permitted to return home to the lake. In return the leaders agreed to settle future grievances with the whites in accordance with the law of the white men. This ended the largest Indian-white confrontation in the area with the Paiutes continuing to live in their ancient home.

The Rush to Washoe, Indian war, and now the establishment of Fort Churchill along the Carson River on the overland trail made 1860 an eventful year. The continued rapid movement of events in the fall of 1860 and spring of 1861 pushed the area swiftly toward a government separate from Utah Territory. The election of the Republican Abraham Lincoln in November of 1860 and the withdrawal of Southern

representatives from Congress cleared the way for the creation of several new territories in the West that had been held back by Southern opposition. The petitions from Roop's local provisional government plus important support from California senators and congressmen brought the passage of the Nevada Organic Act to create Nevada Territory in the final days of President James Buchanan's administration.

To the north of the Comstock and down into the Truckee Meadows, the increased activity in mining saw a quickening of traffic across the Truckee River. It now moved over a rudely constructed bridge owned and built by Charles W. Fuller. Fuller pursued his enterprise after it became clear that the Comstock would expand and grow. The entire valley was attuned to the events in the ore deposits in the mountains to the south. Fuller's bridge was, of course, a toll bridge and appeared a promising enterprise when a road connected Virginia City and the Truckee River in 1861. This road eventually served travelers coming through the Henness Pass-Donner Lake route over the mountains and ranchers transporting foodstuffs to the Comstock from north of the river. Also, the Comstock developed an insatiable demand for lumber and fuel wood. Teamsters from every logging area in the Sierra contracted to haul to the Comstock. One source describes the travel: "Stages rolled swiftly along with their crowds of pas-

San Francisco newspapers in 1868 announced Reno as the future railroad junction between the overland railroad and the yet-to-be-built Virginia and Truckee Railroad to the rich Virginia City mines. Courtesy, Nevada Historical Society

and converted into gold and silver bullion along the Carson River and in Gold Canyon, and the Washoe Valley.

It was during these heady years of Comstock growth that territorial government was established. With the appointment of Orion Clemens as the secretary-treasurer of the new territory came his brother, Samuel Clemens—better known as Mark Twain. In his *Autobiography*, Twain describes Comstock Nevada and some of the experiences of the new territorial governor, James W. Nye. When Nye arrived to assume office, a mischievous attempt was made to humiliate the governor by drawing him into a Western-style drinking bout which, it was hoped, would end in his complete inebriation. But Nye maintained his sobriety, never succumbing to the effects of the liquor he had been lured and cajoled into consuming. His hosts, on the other hand, ended the evening dead drunk under the banquet table.

One of Nye's goals in Nevada was to make the presence of the federal government known and appreciated in a territory whose loyalty to the Union during the Civil War was important. After all, Nevada stood astride the transcontinental transportation and communication lines—the California Trail and the newly constructed telegraph which had replaced the short-lived Pony Express service across the West. And, the gold and silver of the Comstock might be important to the Union should the war be prolonged.

The Comstock remained the focal point of events during the Civil War except when attention turned to Carson City during the legislative sessions in 1861, 1862, and 1864. When the California mining veteran Alf Doten arrived on the Comstock in 1863, he wrote of Virginia City:

Of course it is no use for my pencil to try and describe this place—can't do it—big bustling, noisy city—all in the process of creation—streets full of wagons, horses, omnibusses—sidewalk crowded with rushing crowd—500 houses now being built, mostly wooden but many brick and stone—lots of gambling saloons open to the public—crowded—Monte, faro, chuckerluck, rouge et noir, etc.—bands of music in orchestra—just like San Francisco in '49—in the saloons also were dancing girls—hurdy gurdys, organs, etc. in the street—lots of money flying around in this city.

Although Nevada volunteers were called into the army, a war tax levied, and collections made for the Union Sanitary (hospital) fund, the war was definitely secondary to the main activity of wealth-seeking. In many ways the war isolated Western communities. Most of all it held up the building of a

sengers, while long lines of pack-trains and mule and ox-teams, drawing the capacious prairie schooner, toiled slowly along behind."

In 1861 the shrewd and ambitious businessman, Myron C. Lake, bought the bridge and toll franchise from Fuller. This bridge over the Truckee was known as Lake's Crossing during the rest of the decade. The crossing is recognized as the beginning of the yet-unnamed community of Reno. Lake set about to make improvements by building an inn called Lake House and a more durable bridge. He spent the profit from these enterprises on surrounding land. This was a gamble because who could predict how long the Comstock would last?—or, more importantly, if the transcontinental railroad would ever come through the valley. But apparently Lake believed, correctly, that "the valley was ready for the hand of enterprise."

Meanwhile Comstock development moved ahead, now under the civil government provided by a new territory and in a series of towns along the lode—Silver City, Gold Hill, and the largest, Virginia City. Once brought to the surface the ore had to be processed: thus was a new industry introduced into the area. Wagons hauled ore to mills where it was crushed

Below: James W. Nye served as the first and only governor of Nevada Territory between 1861 and 1864. Appointed by President Abraham Lincoln, he was a strong supporter of the Union during the Civil War. Courtesy, Special Collections Department, Getchell Library, University of Nevada-Reno

Below: Jesse Lee Reno died at the Battle of South Mountain, Maryland, during the Civil War. Judge Edwin B. Crocker, railroad attorney and brother of Charles Crocker, suggested that the new community be named to honor General Reno. Courtesy, Nevada Historical Society

transcontinental railroad which promised so much for Western development. On the other hand, there is little doubt that the war pushed Nevada along to early statehood in October of 1864. Though an area of barely 40,000 people, Nevada was welcomed by the Union government as another loyal state on October 31, 1864 in time for the November Presidential elections.

The end of the war in 1865 unleashed the pent-up energies of America's railroad builders. From Sacramento the Central Pacific built eastward over the mountains and chose the Truckee River Canyon in its approach to the Washoe Country. The Union Pacific built westward from Omaha. The two railroads eventually connected at Promontory Summit, Utah, on May 10, 1869. In western Nevada various communities and mere dots on the map hoped that the road coming over the mountain being built by thousands of Chinese laborers would favor them with a station, or perhaps in the future a major junction. On these decisions by railroad officials hinged the fate of scores of communities.

Myron Lake moved quickly to convince railroad officials to build the main station for the Truckee Meadows near his bridge crossing instead of farther east at Glendale or near present-day Sparks. For the purposes of building a station he deeded Charles Crocker of the railroad 40 acres in March of 1868. In return Crocker agreed to build the depot on these lands and deed back to Lake a number of the lots after they had been surveyed.

On May 9, 1868, the railroad auctioned off 400 town lots. Within a month, over a hundred homes and businesses were established. Myron Lake's gamble with his land investments proved shrewd and personally rewarding. They also secured

the growth of a new community around the railroad, his bridge, and his hotel.

In naming the new depot stops along the route, railroad officials often proved capricious and arbitrary. When they bypassed the high hopes of Crystal Peak by establishing a community a few miles away, they named it Verdi after the Italian opera composer Giuseppe Verdi (local residents promptly called it Ver-dye). The name chosen for Lake's Crossing depot and junction was somewhat more homegrown. It was named after General Jesse L. Reno, who had fallen at the Battle of South Mountain in Maryland in 1862 early in the Civil War. (The family name—Renault—was French, and had been anglicized phonetically.)

Many speculated that the new station on the transcontinental line would be named Argenta (silver), a name thought both melodious and appropriate, and that it would be the largest city between San Francisco and Missouri. Not only was it decided that the depot should be at Lake's Crossing, but also that it should be the junction for any future railroad connecting Virginia City and the transcontinental line that came four years later.

Much of the activity in the Washoe Country now began to shift northward along the Truckee. The Comstock still commanded the region, but many said that the transcontinental railroad would outlast the riches of the mines. In the end those communities that did cast their lots with the railroad survived beyond the glory of the mining metropolis. As it was, Reno, or "Raino" as many pronounced it, took root in the more stable ground of transportation and commerce, not in the spectacular but ephemeral wealth of the precious-metals industry.

These Paiute Indians were photographed in 1889. Describing Reno in August 1868 a San Francisco Times *correspondent wrote, "Reno is a mushroom town . . . mixed stages of civilization from the Paiute squaws with juvenile encumbrances packed neatly in small packages on their broad backs . . . people rush into Reno." Courtesy, Nevada Historical Society*

Below: Washoe Indian women are seen here washing clothes at one of the hot springs in the Truckee Meadows, probably very close to Moana Springs. Courtesy, Nevada Historical Society

Bottom: Paiute communities developed at the edges of hay fields as men's roles changed from hunting to field work by the 1880s. This traditional sunshade and house was formed with willows gathered along the rivers. Courtesy, Nevada Historical Society

CHAPTER TWO

RENO OUTLIVES THE COMSTOCK

For the first decade of its life Reno stood in the shadows of the dazzling events on the Comstock. But the decline of the lode offered opportunities to those who were able to endure the following 20-year depression from 1880 to 1900.

Growth in the "tough little town by the Truckee" was slow over the next two decades. From just over 1,000 people in 1880 Reno grew to 3,500 in 1890 and to 4,500 in 1900. This slow but sustained growth occurred during the midst of a statewide depression that saw the state's population fall from 62,266 in 1880 to 42,335 in 1900, or a loss of nearly 35 percent of its population. These 20 years of depression froze Nevada and its surviving communities into the social and political mold of the late 19th century. While neighboring states urbanized, vastly increased their population, and moved confidently ahead toward the 20th century with industrial and agricultural development, Nevada and its communities lingered in the shadows of its past. A poverty of human and material resources stood at the root of Nevada's problem. Those who were kind described the state, with its relics of decaying mining towns, as "quaint." Others, not so kind, spoke of revoking Nevada's statehood. In response Nevadans embraced almost any cause to salvage their fortunes and communities—Free Silver, irrigation, the annexation of adjacent territories, legalization of boxing, and the beginning of a divorce business.

Through all of this Reno lived on, and some would even say prospered. The absentee ownership of the Comstock mines and mills by San Francisco corporations was mirrored in railroad communities like Reno where the Central Pacific was a major industry, controlled also from California. Despite the colonial status of Nevada's economic development as a way station and precious-metals mining area, boosterism and faith in the future persisted.

Aggressive leaders in Reno saw the town as the new seat of Washoe County. The current seat of county government was in Washoe City, in the valley between Carson City and Reno.

Old Washoe City had prospered by supplying lumber to the Comstock and milling its ores. The challenge from the new town by the Truckee showed that Reno pinned its hopes on railroad development favoring its future. Already by 1869 work began to connect the Comstock with Reno by rail when construction started on the Virginia and Truckee (V&T) Railroad under the direction of Comstock banking and mining mogul William Sharon. The completion of this railroad down the canyons from the Comstock to Carson City and then north to Reno through the Washoe Valley in 1872 radically altered the economy of Washoe City. The new rails enabled milling works for the mines to shift to points along its route in the canyons and along the Carson River. When the tracks came through Washoe Valley not even a depot was built in Washoe City. That honor in the valley was conferred upon Franktown.

Any hope that Washoe City might have had for future growth and prominence was shattered by that decision. The doors of businesses, such as John Richardson's Toe Jam Saloon and even the county courthouse, would soon be closed. The same was true of other Washoe Valley communities—Galena, Ophir, and even Franktown did not prosper. The valley's future would be neither urban nor industrial. This valley that linked the Truckee Meadows with Carson City became a beautiful rural haven marked by the Victorian architecture of the Winters Ranch and the extravagant granite mansion of Sandy Bowers and his wife, Eilley Orrum Bowers. Their rich claims on the Comstock seemed to produce a boundless source of wealth which enabled the Bowers to travel throughout Europe buying treasures for their castle-like residence in Washoe Valley. But the Bowers' riches played out: the fine mansion's furnishings were sold, and the structure itself abandoned. Sandy went to an early grave and Eilley struggled to survive by telling the fortunes of gullible miners. The empty shell of the mansion in the valley testified to the fickle winds of fate that blew almost every day like the

Constructed in 1868, the Depot Hotel was the first and finest hostelry in
town for many years. Burned to the ground in 1879, the hotel was rebuilt,
operating until 1889 when another conflagration destroyed it. From
History of Nevada, *Thompson and West, 1881*

Washoe Zephyr throughout this Western mining country.

As both town and family destinies perished in the shifting fortunes of the mining world, Reno moved to secure its position in the Washoe Country. Already the promise had been made that Reno would be the junction for connecting the V&T Railroad to the transcontinental route. Now Reno moved with confidence to claim the county seat and some even voiced rumors of its ambitions on the state capital. Although previously denied, the County Commission approved a transfer of the county seat in 1870 confirming the results of general elections in the county on the question.

Shifting the county seat sparked another controversy within Reno itself. The fortunes of Myron Lake, always a topic of conversation in the town, were again at stake. Lake offered to donate one acre as the site of the new courthouse. But the acre was located on the south side of the river adjacent to other lands owned by the entrepreneur. Most of the town was located on the north side extending outward from the railroad station. In addition Lake agreed to give $1,500 toward the building's construction and supply it with water. Immediately the proposal was denounced as a scheme by Lake to enhance the value of his real estate south of the Truckee. But the offer was too enticing for the county board to refuse. The governing body accepted the offer in the face of loud criti-

cism. Lake predicted that the lots south of the Truckee would eventually become the most fashionable property in the city.

The acceptance of the land was complicated by Lake's struggle to retain a monopoly on bridge traffic across the Truckee. In 1872 the V&T Railroad built its iron bridge

Eilley Orrum Bowers came to the Washoe Valley in 1855. She later married Lemuel "Sandy" Bowers, and the pair became wealthy from the mines of the Comstock Lode. Courtesy, Nevada Historical Society

The $400,000 mansion built by Sandy and Eilley Bowers featured solid granite walls, French plate-glass windows, and gold and silver alloy doorknobs. It is depicted here as H. Behringer painted it in 1893. Courtesy, Nevada Historical Society

servant of the mining empire in the mountains and a point of departure for people who stepped off the transcontinental railroad headed for the bustle and promise of the mining towns and camps in northern Nevada. By 1881 the Nevada California Railroad began building northward from Reno into California. Renamed the Nevada, California, and Oregon (NCO) in 1885, the line stayed on the east side of the mountains eventually reaching Lakeview, Oregon in 1912.

Around these rude economic foundations the niceties of life slowly began to grow up in and near the new muddy and dusty streets of Reno. A temporary public school established in 1868 was replaced in 1869 by the Riverside Schoolhouse in a building costing $3,000. Later early Reno educators Orvis Ring and Mary S. Doten began their local teaching careers at this school which stood for 35 years. Downstream from Reno the Glendale School operated at a trading settlement founded by John F. Stone and Charles C. Gates. The school had opened its doors in April 1864.

Following the schools came the churches, social organizations, fire and police protection, and an active journalistic community. The Methodist Church appeared in 1869; the Catholic in 1870; the Congregational Church in 1873; the Episcopal Church opened in 1875 in conjunction with the opening of Bishop Whitaker's Seminary for Women in 1876. The Dominican Sisters likewise opened a preparatory school, Mt. St. Mary's Academy, in 1877. The Jewish Benevolent Society formed after the disastrous fire in the Reno commercial district in 1879. In the next decade came the Baptist Church in 1882 and the Advent Church in 1887. An Odd Fellows Hall appeared in 1876 and the Masonic Hall in 1873. Volunteer fire departments emerged soon after the establish-

across the river just east of Lake's. Lake protested the use of the bridge by foot and wagon traffic, going so far as to personally block people and their wagons from using it. Meanwhile the county revoked Lake's exclusive franchise to provide toll-bridge service over the river, which had been given by the territorial legislature for a 10-year period beginning in 1861. Lake challenged the move in court, but the revocation stood and Lake's Crossing bridge became a public thoroughfare, much to the disgust of Lake but to the relief of residents who resented Lake's growing prosperity and high toll charges. It was estimated that when Lake died in 1884, he left an estate of over $2 million accumulated from the tolls and reinvestment in real estate and various local businesses. In 1877 the county built an iron bridge across the river to replace Lake's wooden one.

Reno continued to be the crossroads of the Washoe Country. Roads out of the town were appropriately named for their destinations. The main road across Lake's bridge was called Virginia Street because the bulk of its traffic was bound for Virginia City. A street just to the west of Virginia, on which traffic arrived and departed for the Sierra Valley, was named Sierra. After the arrival of the V&T Reno continued to be a

C.C. Powning began his newspaper career as a newsboy. He eventually moved up to the editorship and later ownership of the Nevada State Journal *in 1874. From* History of Nevada, *Thompson and West, 1881*

William F. Edwards, seen here in 1878, purchased with R.L. Fulton the Reno Evening Gazette, *the* Journal's *main competitor, in November 1878. Courtesy, Nevada Historical Society*

ment of Reno with the Reno Hook and Ladder Company.

Newspapers in the 19th century served as the mouthpieces of new communities. Reno's newspapers, although not equaling the Comstock journalistic tradition which saw such personalities as Mark Twain, Dan DeQuille, Wells Drury, and Alf Doten, offered the new community an identity and self-consciousness. *The Eastern Slope* newspaper quickly saw the doom of Washoe City and moved from the community to Reno in 1868 renaming itself the *Reno Crescent*. It lived on as a weekly until its demise in 1875. The *Nevada State Journal* entered the newspaper field in 1870. In 1874 it came under the ownership of rising Reno landowner, businessman, and future state senator C.C. Powning. A competing daily appeared in 1876, the *Reno Evening Gazette*, under the ownership of John F. Alexander. It was eventually purchased by R.L. Fulton and W.F. Edwards; Fulton later became sole owner. Although the paper eventually passed through many ownerships, it generally held to strict Republican party doctrine eschewing even the attractive Silver cause

for Nevada in the 1890s. These two newspapers remained a part of the Reno scene until 1983, when they were merged into the *Reno Gazette-Journal*.

During the 1870s Reno's journalistic community avidly reported developments in the new town. Reno's first baseball club, the Reno Stars, was organized in June 1871; the Reno Glee Club followed in September. In 1875 on the south side of the river and one mile east of Reno, 40 acres of land was designated as the County Poor Farm. A year later a contract was drawn up for the construction of a county hospital on the property. A building for performances appeared in Reno when L.H. Dyer opened the first theater in 1871 to attract some of the larger acting companies heading for the Comstock.

Reno became the site of the state insane asylum when it was built 2.5 miles east of Reno in 1882. Reno nearly obtained the state prison, but the building which commenced in 1874 fell far short of completion amidst rumors of scandal and charges of misappropriated funds. Governor Lewis R.

Below: This Reno grade-school room was captured on film in 1897. Courtesy, Jean C. Hubbard

Bottom: Bishop Whitaker's School for Girls was established by Episcopal Bishop Ozi W. Whitaker in 1876 on the heights overlooking Reno from the northwest. From History of Nevada, Thompson and West, 1881

Bradley believed that the state prison should be moved from Carson City and relocated on the banks of the Truckee to take advantage of the water power in the development of a prison woolen-mills industry. Land was purchased just east of Reno. After the completion of three of the prison walls and the expenditure of $90,711, the legislature refused any further appropriations. For years these stone walls stood near the river, serving as an occasional ice rink in cold winters. Gradually they crumbled or were disassembled for their building materials by enterprising residents. And Carson City breathed easier as it became apparent that it would retain both the state prison and the state capital and not forfeit them to the ambitions of Reno. Reno's continued drive for additional state institutions was finally rewarded in 1885 when the legislature transferred the struggling beginnings of a state university from Elko to land north of Reno's town center.

The last year of the 1870s was a dramatic and discouraging time for Reno. In March 1879 a disastrous fire fanned by the Zephyr-like winds from the Sierra swept through 10 blocks of

Below: Horse and buggy days in Reno demanded the services of blacksmith shops such as this one. Courtesy, Nevada Historical Society

Bottom: Constructed between 1872 and 1873, the first Washoe County Court House served the people of Reno until 1911. Courtesy, Nevada Historical Society

the downtown destroying 350 buildings. There was almost a million dollars in property losses and six lives were lost. In August trouble erupted in the Chinese community along "Confucius Avenue" adjacent to the east side of town.

The Chinese, who had been brought to Nevada to build the transcontinental railroad, stayed on in the country taking whatever jobs they could get after the railroad was com-

pleted. In the hard times after the failure of the Comstock, the Chinese came under attack in Nevada and California because their willingness to work for lower wages threatened the livelihoods of white workers. When a Chinese firm won the contract to build the Truckee-Steamboat Springs irrigation canal, feelings ran high against the Chinese in Reno. The newly formed Workingmens Club protested the contract and one evening in early August the Chinese section of the city burned. Rumors suggested that the quarter was either permitted to burn or was deliberately torched. Many in the Chinese community evacuated Reno as the rest of the town waited in fear of reprisals from the "celestials." But no violence occurred.

Reno had not yet addressed adequately the question of law and order. A public hanging of a convicted murderer occurred at the Court House in 1878. Yet Reno possessed no local town government until after the turn of the century. Although the town considered itself an incorporated entity since 1876, it was governed by the County Board which did not appoint a police chief until 1889. In the absence of local law enforcement, citizens by the mid-1870s formed a 601 Vigilante Committee. Already a similar committee had

The "white winter" of 1890 blanketed Reno with snow, destroying the open-range cattle industry in the eastern portion of the state. Courtesy, Nevada Historical Society

appeared on the Comstock, copying other vigilante movements in Montana and San Francisco. (Explanations of the origins of this name vary, but supposedly the groups were made up of 600 good citizens and the one who identified and "got the goods" on the victim.) The widespread existence of vigilantes under this common name of the 601 Committee indicated how interlaced were the West's popular responses to lawlessness. In many communities and even on the Comstock the 601 Committees claimed responsibility for lynchings, but in Reno its activities were confined to issuing "tickets of leave" and an occasional tar-and-feathering of individuals deemed undesirable. Quasi-military or rifle organizations called the Reno Guard and Ulster Guards added to the force of extra-legal justice in the town.

By 1881 self-appointed enforcers of public morality and decency came under fire in the town's press. Harassment of the Chinese by those claiming to be members of the 601 Committee became a sore issue which led to the disappearance of the Committee until it re-emerged briefly in 1899. In the one lynching that did take place in Reno in 1891, the 601 Committee was not implicated. Luis Ortíz, in the early morning of September 19, 1891, was hanged from the steel bridge

across the Truckee by a group of 75 men. Previously 12 masked men had forced their way into the jail and escorted Ortíz to the bridge. A day before the victim had severely wounded a popular deputy and on another occasion was accused of killing a man in Reno. The coroner gave the usual pronouncement in such cases: "Death at the hands of persons unknown."

By the 1890s Reno was midway through the 20-year depression gripping the state. It had experienced fire, anti-Chinese protests, vigilante actions, and even a brief visit from ex-President Grant in the gloomy fall of 1879. The State Fair began in Reno in 1874 and in 1885 the state purchased 80 acres for a permanent fairgrounds adjacent to the university's land. The new facility was to be managed by the state Agricultural Association. This association underlined the quest by Nevadans to slow the exodus of population and to find a stable industry to attract a permanent population. Reno became the center for such new thinking about the future of Nevada—a future that did not look to the promises of mining riches. Unfortunately one of the state's sources of wealth outside of mining had just met with disaster in the "white winter" of 1890. The winter wiped out 80 to 90 percent of the cattle on the open range across the northern and eastern part of the state, blocked rail traffic, and generally added to the misery in the depression-struck state.

One new resident of the state was not at all despairing of its future as he traveled to Reno by rail across the storm-ravaged lands in the spring of 1891. In the view of Francis G. Newlands the hard winter brought snows to the mountains that could be stored in reservoirs and used to develop Nevada's agricultural potential. Frank Newlands had become rich through his association with Comstock millionaire William Sharon, whose daughter he had married in 1874. Both Sharon and his daughter were now dead, but Newlands was executor of the vast estate. His decision to move to Nevada in 1888 from his residence in San Francisco caused excitement in the Nevada press. His departure from California occurred after his failure to win high political office there. In Nevada he intended "to pursue [his] career," which undoubtedly meant politics.

Newlands chose Reno for his new home. On land overlooking the Truckee in 1891, Newlands built a fine home in the style of the Queen Anne period and surrounded it with an orchard. Recently remarried, he determined that this new home would be a symbol of his dedication to the future of Reno and the state. His investment in the building itself would, he hoped, put to rest charges that he only wished to buy a U.S. Senate seat from Nevada and then live outside of the state, as many other Nevada senators, including Sharon, had done.

Newlands' arrival brought new energy to Reno. He saw the little town growing into a beautiful intermountain city with a busy promenade along the banks of the dashing, sparkling waters of the Truckee. He urged the community to undertake the investment in dam and reservoir sites in the mountains in order to lay the foundation for what he saw as the greatness of the region's agricultural potential. Much to the disbelief of many Nevadans, he announced that the era of mining had passed in the state and should be replaced by the era of irrigated agriculture which would provide for stable economic growth and lay the foundation for greater commerce and even manufactures.

Newlands first urged Washoe County, then the state, to undertake the work, but all of these efforts failed in the poverty of Nevada life in the 1890s. Critics from the eastern part of the state charged that only Reno would benefit from such plans. Reno newspapers dismissed such allegations and referred to their complaints as mutterings from the "ignorami of the alkali flats." When it became apparent that local government would not act on the proposals, Newlands himself

Making his home in Reno, Francis G. Newlands became known as a progressive Western senator after his election to the United States Senate in 1903. Courtesy, Nevada Historical Society

bought reservoir sites, one of which was Donner Lake, to hold until the community could raise the funds for purchase. Again this reflected his belief in the growth of Reno and the Truckee Meadows. In 1892 he became Nevada's representative in Congress marking the beginning of 10 years in this office before he was able to fulfill his aspirations of obtaining a senatorial seat in 1903.

While Reno struggled, and largely failed, to meet the challenges that its richest citizen proposed, the winds of a new political movement called the Silver Party began to disrupt stable politics in the community. The Silverites formed Silver Clubs and demanded that silver money be coined by the federal government on an unlimited basis to increase the money supply and incidentally raise the demand and price of silver. Nevadans believed that a higher price for silver would enable mines all over the state to reopen. The end of the depression would be at hand. Although the silver cause won Nevada, Reno as a community refused to climb completely aboard the Silver Party bandwagon. When national defeat of the movement in the Presidential election of 1896 indicated the hopelessness of the cause, Renoites could smugly congratulate themselves on resisting total infatuation with the lost cause.

The tendency for Nevadans to champion cure-alls for their economic plight indicated the desperation many citizens felt

Machine shop workers for the Nevada, California, and Oregon Railroad are seen here in 1901. The NCO connected Reno to Lakeview, Oregon, by 1912. Courtesy, Nevada Historical Society

in the depths of this depression. After 1893 Nevada's depression was compounded by a national depression that brought many of Newlands' development plans for urban growth and beautification to a halt. Many of the problems of a small city had to be confronted, however: towns even of small size had to have electricity, gas, water, sewage, streetcars, and telephones. By the end of the century Reno tried to face up to these demands. One resident of the city by the name of Frank Bell, cousin of telephone inventor Alexander Graham Bell, introduced the telephone to Reno in 1881 when he connected his home to C.C. Powning's. The Reno Gas Company started delivering manufactured gas to homes and businesses as early as 1876; this was followed by the Reno Electric Light and Power Company, which delivered steam-generated power by 1882. Several franchises were offered to companies to build a streetcar system and one was taken up by Newlands, but the difficult times discouraged the notion of streetcar transportation for the city. Water and sewage problems from the very beginning of growth in the Truckee Meadows demanded attention. Sewage for the most part ran directly into the Truckee. This practice had to be curbed, especially in the view of Newlands, who saw the river as indispensable to Reno's future.

By the late 1880s Renoites had begun complaining about pollution of the river from upstream sawmills. Reno doctors charged that dumping sawdust in the stream contributed to epidemics of typhoid and sportsmen complained of destruction of the river's trout run. Mill operators in Floriston, California countered that sawdust did not contaminate the river and that Reno's water problems sprang from an 11-mile-long open ditch from its reservoir to the town. By 1889, with the decline of the sawmill industry along the river, the state legislatures of Nevada and California passed laws prohibiting the dumping of sawdust into rivers. As this issue subsided a related one arose when a pulp mill began operations at Floriston in 1898-1899. The Truckee was never to be fully protected against its pollutants, but by 1908 Reno began receiving drinking water from the Hunter Creek Reservoir in the mountains south of the Truckee.

As early as the 1880s Reno was advertised by railroad brochures as a beautiful sanatorium in the mountains boasting hot mineral springs in several parts of the valley and air which was "a specific for asthma." With all of its advantages, Reno still suffered in this period from the economic depression and also from the competition of San Francisco merchants who used cheaper railroad rates to compete with local merchandisers. Such competition often promoted "buy local" campaigns, but they were never completely successful.

Working in favor of the California trade centers were the railroad transportation rates, which were skewed in favor of San Francisco. Goods could be shipped more cheaply from the East to San Francisco than to Reno. Also, business associations in San Francisco pressured the railroad to charge higher rates for those goods shipped from Reno that competed with San Francisco products. A glaring example of this occurred when Truckee Meadows ranchers began butchering their animals in Reno for reshipment to Bay Area markets. Under pressure from the San Francisco Butchers' Association and Board of Trade, the railroad raised freight rates on the butchered meat, causing the venture to fail in Reno.

All of these discouragements blocked progress in the Truckee Meadows in the closing years of the century. Reno was partly a victim of these unfortunate times, and partly a beneficiary. While the wheels of progress remained stuck in the mire of Nevada's 20-year depression and dwindling population, there emerged certain rewards and bright spots. By the 1890s the economy was basically a small, rural cattle-and-transportation concern on the periphery of more modern urban growth in California and surrounding states. True, Reno became more important as the mining on the Comstock faded; but Reno still suffered from the general stagnation and dismantling of the mining economy. As this situation persisted, Reno and Nevada became fixed in old frontier time and social attitudes. One result was that laws did not change at the rate they did in other states. By the time the 20th century arrived the state and its communities were in some respects outdated and even anachronisms. But in this arrested development that Nevada and Reno experienced, the city and the state would find much of their 20th-century identity.

Of particular importance were the divorce laws which remained unchanged since the territorial period. Reno, without realizing it, stood on the verge of realizing recognition—and even a degree of prosperity—by becoming a divorce center of the nation in the first decade of the new century.

CHAPTER THREE

GOOD TIMES AT LAST

As the 20th century appeared, promoters of growth and modernization in Reno hoped the rough-hewn life of the frontier was behind them. The first decade of the new century saw a dramatic transformation of the town: It grew in population from 4,500 in 1900 to 10,867 in 1910—an increase of roughly 140 percent. Population in Washoe County increased from 9,141 to 17,434, but clearly the bulk of the population growth occurred in Reno.

The town was on the verge of once again benefiting from a mining boom that would revive the high times of the Comstock era. In a remote area 250 miles southeast of Reno, erstwhile prospector and rancher Jim Butler discovered rich ore in the summer of 1900. From this find would grow the new camp of Tonopah and two years later another strike in the same vicinity sparked the growth of Goldfield. Both communities temporarily surpassed Reno's population, but declined as their ore bodies played out by 1910 and afterwards. As during the Comstock, Reno emerged as the important supply town. In the wake of the declining Alaskan gold rush after the turn of the century, some of the new mines were dubbed the "Southern Klondike" and Reno became the jumping-off place for the fortune seekers. Tonopah, Goldfield, and a late-comer, Rhyolite, attracted at least 50,000 people to the state.

In addition to this 20th century mining boom, the desert valleys east of Reno became the site of federally backed irrigation farming. In 1902 Congress passed the National Reclamation Act which Congressman Frank Newlands had so long advocated. In the next year one of the earliest reclamation projects began in Fallon. Reno reaped many of the resulting rewards of an economic upswing that boosted spirits and optimism after long years of depression. To those who had stayed on, the promises about the return of growth and prosperity were at hand.

With the good times, Reno connected the development in the outlying desert and mountain valleys of Nevada to the world of commerce, finance, and industry in San Francisco and the East. New enterprise in precious metals mining, agriculture, and even copper mining in far-off White Pine County in eastern Nevada were good omens for Reno. Hand in hand with prosperity in the city came renewed interest in civic improvements, educational concerns, city government, and campaigns to bring Reno up to date in the 20th century. Since 1876 Reno had considered itself an incorporated town, but still it was governed by the county commissioners who had power to prohibit nuisances, levy taxes, and pass ordinances to regulate fire and police departments. The 1897 legislature gave more home rule to Reno's local government, but reneged on the action in the 1899 session.

It was not until 1903 that the legislature made up its mind to grant full-fledged city government to Reno. Municipal government arrived at a time when cities throughout America began to experiment with new forms of city government. City-manager-style governments and commission forms of government arose, but Reno adhered to the traditional mayor-council government whereby council members were elected from defined geographical areas, or wards, within the town. Reno's first mayor was D.W. O'Conner. In 1907 the talented and ambitious Richard Kirman (banker and future governor of the state by 1934) was elected in the city-wide mayoral elections along with five elected ward members. Reno city government included not only a mayor and council members, but also a city court, city engineer, city clerk, city auditor, treasurer, chief of police, captain of police, eight policemen, an assessor, city attorney, superintendent of streets, coronor, and public administrator. Reno could boast of a city government administration equal to any city of comparable size in the country.

Throughout the nation a Progressive reform movement touched many local governments, causing them to adopt the innovative forms of city-manager and commission governments. Impelled by the desire to root out corruption

The University of Nevada graduating class of 1891 included Frank Norcross (left), who helped form the Reno Library Association. Courtesy, Nevada Historical Society

A group of Reno's fire fighters was captured by a photographer in the midst of a drill in 1905. Courtesy, Nevada Historical Society

Bottom: Officials of Reno's incorporated city government moved into this new city hall in 1906. It is seen here located next to the Reno Evening Gazette *building and across the street from the Majestic Theater. Courtesy, Nevada Historical Society*

Below: As the name of this store indicates, Reno was an important supplier to people seeking fortunes in the new mining operations in central Nevada. Courtesy, Nevada Historical Society

and bring government under the control of the people instead of special-interest political machines, some Progressives also sought to pass legislation protecting the ordinary citizen from the vices of drink, gambling, and prostitution. To assume more direct control of their destinies, many city governments assumed the ownership of public utilities in drives for municipal ownership. Electricity, water, gas, and even transportation services became city-owned. This did not occur in Reno. The town had neither the resources nor the need to finance public-utility development. Private companies had come on the scene quite early to provide services.

Mining had created a need for electric power and provided a market for power generated from the swift-flowing Truckee. By 1905 there were four power plants along the river west of Reno. Long power lines carried electricity not just to Reno but also to outlying mining communities on the Comstock, Yerington, and Wabuska, to name but a few. The power companies rushed to serve mining developments, but when

these faded, new customers in the towns were eagerly served. Consequently northwestern Nevada communities enjoyed electrical service long before many other areas of the country with greater populations.

The limitations of private capital and a small service area precluded the development of a large-scale hydroelectric dam on the Truckee. Instead of one giant dam, electric companies diverted water from the Truckee into miles of wooden aquaducts hugging the canyon walls until they finally carried their fast-moving waters into the turbines in power stations at Farad in 1900; Reno power plant in 1901; Washoe plant in 1902; the Fleish plant in 1905; and the Verdi plant canal in 1912. All of these plants were connected in parallel, and fed mining and smelting developments as well as the needs of urban Reno and other communities in northwestern Nevada. The closest effort resembling large-scale hydroelectric development occurred with the building of Lahontan Dam on the Carson River when the federal government developed a reservoir for the Fallon irrigation project. The Derby Dam on the Truckee east of Reno was merely a diversion dam to send water from the river to the Newlands irrigation project.

The early availability of power gave Reno the potential to become a manufacturing center. Various mills already located along the river, such as the Riverside Mills and Reno Milling and Flour Company, pointed in this direction. But the scarcity of raw materials, the high price of frontier labor, and eventually the high price of private power closed off Reno's future as a manufacturing center. The railroad had always held the key to Reno's survival.

In 1906 Congress passed the Hepburn Act, which gave greater powers to the Interstate Commerce Commission to regulate railroad and prevent rate discrimination. In the following year the Nevada legislature established a railroad commission to do the same. Reno hailed the legislation and looked forward to greater justice in railroad rates for its products. Another railroad development that benefited Reno was a decision by the V&T Railroad to extend its lines south of Carson City in 1906 to tap the dairy trade of the Carson Valley in Minden and Gardnerville. The products, of course, flowed north to Reno and even on to San Francisco.

But what did the future hold for Reno beyond its function as a commercial redistribution point? Since the transfer of the university from Elko and the strong leadership of University of Nevada President Joseph E. Stubbs, Reno saw itself as a modest educational and cultural center for the state. In railroad advertisements Reno appeared as a Western hideaway offering health and relaxation. Some Eastern lawyers—and one in particular from New York by the name of W.H.

Joseph Edward Stubbs served as president of the University of Nevada from 1894 to 1914. His strong leadership helped make Reno an educational center. Stubbs was also involved in several reform crusades after the turn of the century. Courtesy, Nevada Historical Society

Schnitzer—saw a far different future for the town. By 1900 it became apparent that the state's lenient divorce law presented opportunities for Reno. Schnitzer placed ads in New York newspapers noting the liberality of the law and the mere six-month residency requirement.

Nevada's divorce law was written by the first territorial legislature in 1861 and had remained essentially unchanged. While many other states tightened their divorce law in the late 19th century in an attempt to protect the permanency of the family, not so Nevada. The state remained immune to much social change after the decline of the Comstock. As a result Nevada emerged into the 20th century with its 19th century divorce law intact. The law provided seven grounds for divorce: desertion; cruelty; non-support; drunkenness; impotence; imprisonment; and adultery.

The 1906 Reno divorce of Laura Corey, wife of U.S. Steel president William E. Corey, attracted notoriety throughout

A poster for the "Fight of the Century" announced the 15-round contest for the Heavyweight Championship of the World held in Reno on July 4, 1910. Jack Johnson (left) successfully defended his title against former champion Jim Jeffries (right) in the fight. Courtesy, Nevada Historical Society

mining communities often hosted the fights after the turn of the century. In 1906 Goldfield cheered the Joe Gans-Oscar Nelson fight. But the most famous contest in Nevada fight history was held in Reno on July 4, 1910. Boxing promoter "Tex" Rickard staged the "Fight of the Century" when he matched the current heavyweight black champion Jack Johnson in a 15-round bout with ex-white champion Jim Jeffries of San Francisco. Publicity went out over the wires to every corner of the nation, billing the fight as a symbolic struggle between the white and black races. Jeffries, who had been in retirement since 1905, was persuaded to come back and be the "Great White Hope."

The fight, originally scheduled to be held in San Francisco, was stopped by an indignant letter-writing campaign against the immorality of boxing and a suggestion to California's Governor J.N. Gillett that San Francisco might not be considered for the Panama Pacific Exposition if the fight occurred. The Governor cancelled the fight in mid-June allowing only two weeks for its relocation. Reno, Goldfield, and Salt Lake City extended invitations. The mayor of Reno assured Rickard that a 20,000-seat stadium could be constructed for the expected crowd. Shortly after the Reno site was announced, Reno's clergy attacked the decision. The Reverend L.H. Burwell of Reno's Methodist Church spoke of "Reno's Disgrace" and said from the pulpit that the fight would demoralize the community and bring "riffraff" and the "offscouring of the country" to Reno. But Nevada's Governor Denver S. Dickerson assured Rickard that no amount of protest by "reformers" could cause the fight's cancellation. Good transportation and the close proximity to California helped Rickard choose Reno. The important hotels—the Riverside, the Overland, and the Golden—soon booked their rooms to capacity.

By the end of June both fight teams set up their training centers. Jeffries established himself at Moana Hot Springs and Johnson at Rick's Resort on the old Verdi Road. The flamboyant Johnson, not surprisingly, was unpopular with the white fight crowd. For the most part the thousands who gathered in a hastily built wooden amphitheater on East 4th Street eagerly looked forward to his ignominious defeat at the hands of Jeffries. But to the crowd's disappointment, Johnson carried the day, defeating the aging Jeffries in 15 long, gruelling rounds. Although the results of the fight were gloomy for the fans, Reno businessmen were elated over their profits. The world was starting to notice Reno—a wild, raucous town in a beautiful mountainous setting where divorce seekers, cowboys, free-flowing liquor, and boxing fans mingled openly in a wide-open society.

the country and the world. By 1910 Reno harbored a well-recognized and publicized "Divorce Colony." Here gathered a transient group waiting out their six-month residencies. The colony provided Reno lawyers with a lucrative business, hotel and dude ranches with guests, and well-stocked department stores with customers demanding the latest fashions for their new start in life. In 1910 popular singer Billy Murray captured the feeling of many would-be divorcés in a new record release entitled, "I'm on My Way to Reno." One verse went:

> *I'm on my way to Reno, I'm leaving town today*
> *Give my regards to all the boys and girls along Broadway*
> *Once I get my liberty, no more wedding bells for me*
> *Shouting the Battle Cry of Freedom.*

Prize fights became another Reno attraction. In an early attempt to encourage tourists, the Nevada legislature legalized "glove contests" in 1897. Almost immediately the James J. Corbett and Bob Fitzsimmons fight in Carson City drew attention to Nevada as a fight center. Rough, booming, new

But Reno was not totally isolated from the forces of reform. Already the 1909 legislature had passed one of the strictest anti-gambling laws in the nation. It did not take effect, however, until October 1, 1910. The fight crowds during July 1910 enjoyed the last summer of free and open gambling until it was again made legal 21 years later. Another reform that was much talked about and advocated in many states was prohibition—Oklahoma had even entered the Union as a dry state in 1907. In a sense Reno became torn between the attraction to reform on the one hand and its own profitable image of a fun-loving and vice-tolerant divorce center of the West on the other. The miners, the ranch hands, and the railroad crews—largely a homeless, transient population—saw Reno in the same light as sailors viewed a port city after many months at sea. It was still the rough little town by the Truckee.

University students were warned to avoid the evils of Reno life, especially the dens of iniquity that offered drink, gambling, and even prostitution along Reno's infamous Lake Street. Many of the most active reformers were women, and even Reno had some. Members of Reno's Women's Christian Temperance Union not only attacked the excesses of liquor use, but also urged strict suppression of prostitution and supported pending legislation in Congress that would be known as the Mann Act making it illegal to transport women across state boundaries for immoral purposes. Mrs. A.E. Hersheiser of the Reno WCTU wrote Nevada Senator Newlands on May 31, 1910 urging his support of the Mann Bill. Mrs. Hersheiser, along with another Reno woman, Anne Martin, were also among the leaders in the fight for women's suffrage in Nevada, which was not achieved until 1914. All of these causes were elemental to the Progressive movement. Needless to say,

Reno became a somewhat uncomfortable participant in this national crusade.

Just how uncomfortable Reno became was demonstrated when the Nevada legislature, under pressure from reform groups, lengthened the divorce residency requirement in the state from six months to one year in 1913. Lawyers complained and hotel keepers and merchants lost business. The commercial community demanded repeal. Reno, they argued, could afford the hostile remarks about rampant and easy divorce: the city would just have to foster the idea of a Reno divorce as a service to society, not a threat to family and community life. Reno should be seen as a harbinger of a new age in which difficult marital problems could be humanely terminated through what was becoming known as "the cure" in Reno.

It did not take long for the Nevada legislature to see the error of its ways, especially when Reno businessmen actively campaigned against legislators supporting the one-year law. The 1915 legislature took immediate steps to restore the six-month residency, but in the process Washoe County legislators were forced to strike a bargain with those from Churchill County. Since the development of the reclamation district in

attached to Progressivism. The argument for Prohibition in wartime was that the grain used to make alcohol was better used as food for the Allies. In November 1918 Nevadans and Renoites voted to ban the sale and manufacture for sale of alcoholic beverages. This meant no beer, no wine, no hard liquor for sale. As Nevada became a dry state, Reno's lucrative liquor business and favorite watering places closed their doors. No doubt without the war effort, the reform movement alone would not have been able to close the doors of Reno's saloons.

However reluctant the reform spirit in Reno, it did display many of the concerns expressed nationally and in other communities. Since the 1890s Reno's leading women's club, the Century Club (later the 20th Century Club), had taken an interest in preschool kindergarten education. From this interest the Reno Kindergarten Association grew, providing preschool experience for Reno's children. By 1901 a two-story brick building housed the Babcock Memorial Kindergarten which was deeded to the Reno Public School District in 1932. In addition to working for educational reforms, women in Reno sought Sunday closing laws, greater regulation of liquor and vice, and of course, the right to vote.

Support for education was particularly crucial in these times of expanding population in the city. Education had never fared too well in Nevada communities where so much of the population consisted of transient males with few family responsibilities. In 1908 Reno's school district issued $100,000 in bonds to build Orvis Ring and McKinley Park schools. They were to be almost exact counterparts—incorporating one-story mission-type architecture with a courtyard surrounded by three sides of schoolrooms. In 1910 the School Board authorized another $250,000 for two more similar grade schools and a high school to be done in the Spanish Renaissance style. The two new grade schools, Mary

Fallon, the people of the district saw it as the agricultural center of Nevada and the proper place for the annual state fair that Reno hosted. Return to the six-month residency rule was made at the price of relocating the state fair in Fallon, where it remained until 1950.

At a price, Reno had won back its lucrative divorce industry. The 1915 legislature also relaxed the strict laws against gambling excepting games of skill, like poker, as opposed to games of pure chance. This opened the way for card and poker parlors in the back streets and alleys. But the reformers would score one more victory before Progressivism faded. American entrance into World War I in April 1917 brought a tremendous outpouring of patriotism in Reno and throughout the country. Reno papers denounced those who opposed the war and the *Reno Evening Gazette* endorsed the suspension of free speech for the duration of the war. On April 3, 1917 its editorial page declared: "The argument that this 'is a free country' and a citizen can say what he pleases must be laid aside in time of war."

The commitment to the war pushed Americans and Nevadans into a wider acceptance of Prohibition as part of the moral reform program that some people had zealously

S. Doten and Mount Rose, would soon join the previous ones with similar architecture and layout. The grade schools became known as "the four sisters."

The Dominican Sisters' parochial school served the community from a substantial brick building erected in 1897 at 243 West 6th Street. In 1907 the school responded to a community emergency by converting itself into a temporary hospital to care for hundreds of children when a chicken pox and measles epidemic struck Reno. In the following year, 1908, services to the sick were continued in these quarters with the establishment of St. Mary's Hospital. Several other centers for the care of the sick and the old had been established in Reno by 1917. Among them were the Crittenden Home, Mount Rose Hospital, and St. George Hospital, but Washoe County Hospital and St. Mary's emerged as the community's main medical centers. The state mental hospital, as it was now called, was still located just east of Reno on Asylum Road.

By 1907 the City Directory remarked, "The day of wooden and light brick structures has passed. In their place are arising four-and-five-story brick, steel and stone buildings, erected with a view to meeting the increasing demands of a permanent community." The plain steel bridge across the Truckee on Virginia Street was replaced with a reinforced steel-and-concrete structure in 1905. In the same year a new Masonic Building arose on First and Virginia streets. It was an impressive brick structure with columns overshadowing the sidewalk along Virginia Street. In 1907 the wooden Riverside Hotel came down to make way for a new impressive brick structure. Reno architect Frederic J. DeLongchamps won the bid for his design of the new Reno Post Office in 1907 and the Washoe County Court House in the heart of downtown Reno in 1910.

Beyond the world of brick, steel, and concrete structures, other Renoites were engaged in movements to establish cultural institutions. Frank Norcross was instrumental in the formation of the Reno Library Association. It sought contributions and held money-raising events, but not until the Andrew Carnegie Foundation announced its support in 1903 were hopes for a solid, permanent library building realized. The new structure arose on the south bank of the Truckee on Virginia Street facing the Riverside Hotel. It was known as the Reno Carnegie Public Library. Another cultural institution made its appearance in Reno when the Nevada Historical Society was organized during a meeting in 1904 on the campus of the University of Nevada. Reno then was a center not only of commercial and agricultural trade, and the beneficiary of the state's mining development, but it also possessed the institutions treasured by those who were more culturally and socially aware.

Despite the emergence of a cultural life and social reform

elements in Reno, Nevada beyond the Truckee Meadows remained a rough, hard-bitten place. Even before 1910, Nevada's southern mining boom began to fade. Many feared that the years ahead would offer a repetition of the depression that followed the Comstock boom. The state's population did drop from 81,875 in 1910 to 77,407 in 1920, but Reno once again demonstrated its vitality by posting a gain of nearly 2,500 over its number in 1910.

In the years of Nevada's 20th-century mining boom many of Reno's brightest and most ambitious citizens dashed to the new mining frontiers in the south—Tonopah, Goldfield, and Rhyolite. Pat McCarran, a future state supreme court justice and U.S. Senator, left to seek his fortune soon after he passed the state bar exams. Others came directly to the mines from out of state, but when the mines began to decline, many made their way back to the one place in the state that showed long-term endurance: Reno. The mining communities experienced quick growth and decline. It was estimated that Goldfield had over 15,000 people in 1907 and 1908, but the census report for 1910 showed only 4,838. The decline was more dramatic for Rhyolite, which went from 5,000 people in 1907 and 1908 to only 675 in 1910. The story was similar for Tonopah, where the population plummeted from 10,000 people at one time to only 3,900 in 1910.

The spectacular growth of Nevada mining in the south also brought conflict that affected the entire state. Goldfield became the sight of a dramatic labor dispute in December of 1907 and January of 1908 that saw the intervention of federal

The Reno Wheelmen reflected the growing popularity of the bicycle as a form of exercise, recreation, and transportation from 1896 to 1909. Bicycle clubs such as the Wheelmen campaigned for improved road conditions across America. Courtesy, Nevada Historical Society

troops. More than any other single event, the presence of federal troops and the subsequent passage of the Nevada State Police Bill by the legislature in January 1908 prompted long-standing resentments in the communities of the state. Reno was no exception. The issues appeared clear-cut. The central figure in the conflict was George Wingfield, who, along with U.S. Senator George Nixon, owned the Goldfield Consolidated Mining Company against which workers went out on strike in November 1907.

The owners charged that legitimate unionism in the mines had been subverted by the intrigue of the radical Industrial Workers of the World (IWW) or "Wobblies." Labor on the other hand countered that the presence of "some Wobblies" gave the owners an excuse to call in troops for the purpose of breaking the entire union movement. This was a conclusion also reached by a specially appointed Presidential commission to investigate the request by the State of Nevada for federal troops in Goldfield. The commission found that no threat to either life or property had existed in the community. President Theodore Roosevelt was outraged with the Governor of Nevada, John Sparks, when he learned of the commission's findings. He threatened to remove federal troops immediately, but acknowledged that feelings were running so high in the community that the move would be followed by violence. The solution was to have federal forces replaced by a state police force. Finally the governor was badgered into calling a special session of the legislature whose main order of business was to pass a Nevada State Police Bill.

The bill was widely regarded by labor as a state strike-breaking paramilitary force. In management and business circles it was seen as a force for law and order and protection against radical unionism. Numerous attempts to repeal the Police Bill occurred and no organization was more active in the campaign against repeal than the Reno Commercial Club. Washoe County and Reno represented a conservative, and some would even say anti-labor, voting bloc in the state. When labor's adversary George Wingfield moved to Reno in 1908, he set a trend that others followed. Shortly afterwards Nevada's U.S. Senator George Nixon chose to build a huge double-story, Spanish-style home in Reno that dwarfed the earlier Newlands residence. Clearly all of these moves meant a transference of power in the state back to Reno from the transient mining towns. Significantly these mining kings of the southern fields (Wingfield and Nixon) stayed on in Reno instead of migrating to San Francisco, as many of the wealthy figures of the Comstock had done.

When both the rich and the poor refugees from the mining towns returned to Reno, they brought with them many of the controversies that had plagued the mining camps. Wingfield

The Southern Pacific Company proudly displayed its low rates to Nevada in this 1916 advertisement. Courtesy, Nevada Historical Society

This turn-of-the-century view of Virginia Street features electric lights hanging over the street, heralding progress and prosperity for the city. Courtesy, Nevada Historical Society

and McCarran had become bitter enemies in the south and they continued this long-standing feud for many years as their paths crossed in Reno. Wingfield brought his anti-labor bias and a firm view that people of great wealth must carry influence in political circles. Eventually from his office in room 201 of the Reno National Bank building he became the king-pin in a statewide political machine that called the shots in both of Nevada's political parties. More importantly, many of these new arrivals in town brought wealth, enterprise, and talent back to Reno. Already Wingfield had bought the Golden Hotel in 1907 and would invest heavily in statewide banking from his home base in Reno. Both Nixon and Wingfield established the Nixon National Bank of Reno in October of 1906 while developing their other banking and mining properties in Goldfield.

Reno's banking responded to local conditions and national trends. The advent of the Nixon-Wingfield money into the community's banking picture not only widened its scope, but also added a more adventurous element which supplemented its investments in Nevada mining with those in agriculture, especially livestock agriculture. Ever since D.A. Bender headed the Bender and Company Bankers from 1871 to 1880, banking in the quiet economy of depression Nevada was a subdued affair. First National Bank of Reno was merged with G.W. Mapes' Washoe County Bank under that name in 1896, temporarily leaving Reno without a national bank. In 1903 the Farmers and Merchants National Bank filled the void and came under the presidency of prominent Renoite Richard Kirman from 1904 to 1933. The bank

changed its name to First National Bank in Reno in 1929 and First National Bank or (FNB) in 1934. When George Nixon died in June of 1912, Wingfield became president of the Nixon National Bank and in 1915 its name was changed to Reno National Bank.

The commercial expansion of Reno was also helped by the founding of a neighboring city in 1904. In that year the Southern Pacific Railroad decided to move its main repair shops from Wadsworth, 30 miles east of Reno, to a new community next door which would be named after Governor John Sparks. The new community of nearly 1,000 people just east of Reno and the expansion of the town southward made Reno an ideal place for the building of an urban trolley system.

Bottom: The Nevada Transit Company opened the state's first electric trolley service between Reno and Sparks on Thanksgiving Day, November 24, 1904. The line served Reno and Sparks until 1927. Courtesy, Nevada Historical Society

In 1904 Reno was connected with Sparks by an electric interurban railway that eventually reached out to the new resort south of Reno, Moana Hot Springs. The resort, whose Hawaiian name was chosen by one of the developers, featured baths and a swimming pool fed by natural hot springs which had long been prominent in the area. Two other resorts built on hot springs were at Steamboat Springs and Reno Hot Springs, south of Reno on the way to Carson City, and Lawton (or Laughton) Hot Springs west of Reno. Steamboat Springs had been used during the Comstock era as a favorite health resort. Another favorite place for Renoites was Lake Tahoe, whose shores provided welcome relief in summer. Closer to home, people entertained themselves at the Coney Island amusement park between Reno and Sparks

and at Belle Isle, in the middle of the Truckee in downtown Reno.

Life in Reno was becoming more diversified, as were the people who lived in it. The war spurred the production of livestock and the expansion of ranching, one factor which encouraged the immigration of Basque sheepherders to the mountain pastures of western Nevada. Reno became a gathering point for these 20th-century immigrants. They fol-

lowed Italian immigrants who had become prosperous landowners and potato farmers by the turn of the century. Local Indian labor was widely utilized on the ranches and Indian women came to town in search of domestic work. In an attempt to end some of the enforced isolation of the reservations, the federal government in 1917 acquired 20 acres in Reno to found the Reno-Sparks Indian Colony that offered Nevada Indians homes in the city. An event that reduced the already declining Chinese population in Reno was the ordered evacuation and torching of Chinatown along Lake Street by the city Health Department in 1908. The varied ethnic patterns in the small city were also apparent with the organization in Reno of the African Methodist Episcopal (A.M.E.) Church to serve Reno's small black population. Separation of the races in church also extended to the train depot that designated separate waiting areas for blacks.

Oftentimes the crisis of war brings people together, but on many fronts the entrance of the United States into World War I increased suspicion and even hatred among Americans, provoking the persecution of minority groups. Suspicion surrounded eastern European and German immigrants as their loyalty to the war effort was questioned. In Nevada, Lutheran churches in Minden and Gardnerville suspended the use of the German language in their services. Patriotic groups guarded against disloyalty and declared that new immigrants should seek "Americanization education." These sentiments came to the fore during the war and continued afterwards as several West Coast states passed alien land laws attempting

Moana Springs opened as a resort in October 1905. In addition to a swimming pool heated by natural hot springs, Moana featured a small lake complete with a boating facility and a baseball field. The name is Hawaiian, chosen by an early owner who had visited a similar resort in the Hawaiian Islands. Courtesy, Nevada Historical Society

to prevent the Japanese from owning land.

In 1921 the Reno Bar Association urged the Nevada legislature to eliminate from the state constitution a provision guaranteeing that non-citizens could own property in the state on an equal basis with native-born citizens. This would open the way for the legislature to pass alien land laws similar to California's. In the meantime the *Reno Evening Gazette* could only announce, "Anti-Jap Plan Marking Time." The Ku Klux Klan also made brief appearances in Reno as it did in other communities in the state and nation after the war. These events were a part of the extreme and often mean-spirited nationalism—even xenophobia—which Americans felt in the aftermath of the horrendous European war. Isolationism was the mood of the time. In addition, the Nevada legislature in 1919 prohibited black boxers from fighting white boxers. When Reno fight promoters began talking of bringing two prominent boxers, one black and the other white, to Reno in 1921 for an event similar to the Johnson-Jeffries bout, Reno newspapers told the citizenry to "read the law and weep."

The end of the war and the beginning of the 1920s saw a

Reno imposing greater restrictions on its citizens. Fear of radical labor unions such as the IWW, which had opposed the war, brought anti-labor laws which Reno's business and professional community applauded during the national "Red Scare" in 1919. During it, many people feared the spread of the recent Bolshevik revolution in Russia into the ranks of American labor. In 1920 the nation officially went "dry," mandated by the 18th Amendment to the Constitution. Now laws both locally and nationally prohibited the sale of alcoholic beverages. Prohibition had come to a town that had long been known as a wide-open meeting place for cowboys, sheepherders, ranchers, and miners. While prostitution had come under attack from reformers, it still retained its downtown red-light district after the war which successive presidents of the University of Nevada deplored.

Another industry remained untouched and thriving following the Progressive reform era and the war. Divorce, Reno style, continued to capture the national spotlight as thousands each year made their way to Reno to seek "the cure." Despite restrictive legislation against gambling and drink, Reno was still Reno.

CHAPTER FOUR

RENO AT THE CROSSROADS

The decades between the world wars shaped Reno's 20th-century character in a manner far surpassing any previous experiences. Until this time two choices were open to the city. The first embraced the city's desire to improve urban life by restricting vices and imposing stricter regulations on gambling, drinking, and prostitution. The second fed upon Reno's desire for profits and commercial success. Why a reformed city and commercial success could not coexist in the same town was probably a testimony to the poverty of resources surrounding Reno in the bleak but beautiful state of Nevada. But the choice that Reno would make was by no means clear at the end of the war and as the 1920s began. The fires of reform still glowed in the hearts and minds of many of the city's prominent residents although the war and subsequent postwar depression did much to cool the embers.

Disillusion with the war and the ideals that inspired it also produced a disillusionment with Progressive reform at home. The economic slump after the war, fears of aliens, racial riots in many cities, and the protests of radical labor punctured many dreams about an American people marching toward community progress on the basis of a homogeneous and just society. The ideals of community reform and uplift became lost causes in the general outcry for a "return of normalcy" as Presidential candidate Warren G. Harding termed it in the 1920 election. To many this attractive phrase merely meant a reassertion of self-interests over community interests.

Probably more quickly than other Americans, Renoites tired of causes that sought to protect people from the weaknesses of their own character—penchants for gambling, drinking, disorganized family life, and even prostitution. A sparkling pure city simply was not good business for this mountain and desert center that entertained miners and cowboys and promoted a flourishing divorce industry. Reno of all American towns stood at a difficult crossroads in its history. It had been the focal point of urban growth in the state for the past 20 years and also of the state's weak Progressive reform movement. Reform in Reno as in Nevada had experienced rough sledding. Gambling had been curtailed, not abolished; divorce, prostitution, and drinking survived to taunt the reformers. Statewide prohibition had been accepted only at the last minute under the pressure of wartime necessity in 1918.

As the decade began for Reno the U.S. Census of 1920 revealed that for the first time in American history the majority of the U.S. population lived in cities. In Nevada as on the mining frontier in general the majority of people had always lived in urban settings. The rise of a newer urban America ultimately brought greater freedom to individuals and a shift away from many of the rural values of white Protestant America that the moralistic side of Progressivism had brought to the cities. In the Nevada setting Reno life had never been greatly restrained by these values. As the new urban America sought greater freedom in marriage laws, and ultimately in drinking and gambling, Reno stood ready to respond without many traditional qualms of conscience.

Local politics are often a barometer of the storms of change and discord in communities. From 1919 to 1923 city government was under the mildly reform leadership of Mayor H.E. Stewart. The mayor stood for civic improvement in the paving of streets, the acquisition of parks, and the building of schools.

In acquiring prized park land the city was very successful from 1920 to 1923. Prominent banker and mining entrepreneur George Wingfield deeded to the city Belle Isle, an island in the Truckee in downtown Reno with some additional surrounding land. This would become Reno's quiet and green Wingfield Park. The late Senator Francis G. Newlands, who had died in late 1917, also became an indirect benefactor of city parks when his nephew, James Newlands, sold 49 acres along the Truckee and near a power dam that would eventually be named, in a city-wide contest, Idlewild Park. In the final year of Mayor Stewart's term the Newlands Company gave one acre of land on Newlands

The Reno Order of Camels, a statewide anti-prohibition organization, was founded to combat the anti-liquor laws which had become a feature of Nevada life in 1918. Courtesy, Nevada Historical Society

Opposite: The 1920 July Fourth Reno Rodeo attracted the talent of Western artist Will James. This sketch appeared on many subsequent posters advertising one of Reno's most important tourist weekends during the summer months. Courtesy, Nevada Historical Society

Below: The aftermath of the March 1922 fire which destroyed the Riverside Hotel is depicted here. George Wingfield bought the site in 1924 and construction began in 1925. The present hotel opened in 1927 and subsequently became a favorite with Reno's divorce colony. Courtesy, Nevada Historical Society

Heights overlooking the city for an additional park.

Although both Wingfield and Senator Newlands were benefactors of the city, the two men represented strikingly different traditions in the life of the city; these traditions would clash in the upcoming mayoral elections in 1923. Newlands had grand visions for Reno as the hub of an expanding agricultural and industrial development in western Nevada. Not only would the city nourish commerce, but also education, the arts, civic pride, and beauty. It would be the leader of a reform movement that would remake Nevada into Newlands' much-hoped-for "model commonwealth."

Wingfield, on the other hand, was a shrewd self-made millionaire of Nevada's 20th-century mining boom. He schemed and fought to increase that wealth and protect it from all challengers—labor, reformers, and state taxation. His investments sought out what Nevada had to offer—mining, real estate, hotels, and ranching. He had only one yardstick by which he measured the activities of society or the nature of his investments: if it made money, it was legitimate from his viewpoint.

It was between these two points of view that Reno would choose in 1923. The Newlands tradition represented community regulation, repression of vice, and open democratic politics; the Wingfield tradition sought freedom from restraints, no enforced public morality, and closed machine politics. No hypocrisy there: Wingfield was a gambler, a drinker, and a divorcé.

The move that earned Mayor Stewart the "reform" label was his support of the "Redlight Abatement Movement" which sought to abolish Reno's "restricted district." Long a part of the Reno scene, the prostitution area was briefly closed down during World War I, but immediately reopened afterwards. Two months prior to the election the mayor and his council closed down the "restricted district" and cracked down on the speakeasies which operated almost openly in Reno. The mayoral elections of May 1923 became a referendum on the reform policies of Mayor Stewart. The mayor campaigned under the slogan, "Reno Beautiful Not Reno Notorious." Generally the press expected Stewart's reelection, but acknowledged that a word-of-mouth campaign against the mayor's reforms could be heard on every street corner in the business districts. It was also no secret that Wingfield, the powerful manipulator of Nevada politics, was opposed to Stewart's policies.

Others argued that Reno's commercial progress demanded the abolishment of the red-light district, and for practical reasons, the city council and mayor concurred there would ultimately be more profit for a clean and beautiful city than for a dirty one. Stewart's main campaign issue was the tight restriction of prostitution, reminding voters that "a town run by a tenderloin district is no good." Opposition ads branded Stewart a "reformer" and spoke of Reno as a town with a live-and-let-live attitude, "until the professional reformer came to stir up discontent and turmoil in our midst."

The race for mayor was a three-way contest. Frank Byington was known to have views similar to Stewart's, but the third candidate, E.E. Roberts, dropped strong hints that he had nothing but contempt for the city's efforts to enforce morality. *The Nevada State Journal* said Roberts, a divorce lawyer, had a reputation for frontier ethics and that he was out of step with public opinion when he proposed remaking Reno into a wide-open mining camp. But Roberts openly declared in his campaign:

I don't believe in prohibition or any kind of reform that takes from any man or woman their right to find happiness in their own way. I would repeal all blue laws, I would make Reno the playground of the world.

By election day, May 8, 1923, the *Journal*, which had backed Stewart, admitted that his chance of victory was slight. It admitted that the "open or closed" issue had surpassed in importance the "city beautiful" plea of Stewart. The reform element cried that an "open city" would mean ruin for Reno and the "unreformed" retorted that Reno would be damned if it were not opened up. "Redlights and Prosperity," said the paper, was heard around many business corners, while reform groups such as the Monday Club, Reno League of Women Voters, Reno Women's Christian Temperance Union, the PTA, the Women's Faculty Club, the Reno Lions Club, and various church groups believed in the slogan "Redlights and Ruin" for the town.

The ballot count brought a stunning defeat for Stewart and Byington. Reno had opted for an "unreformed" city, the frontier ethics of Roberts, and the grab-the-profits attitude of Wingfield. Voters had rejected the planned, regulated society of the Newlands tradition. The vote was Roberts, 2,928;

Below: George Wingfield was a central figure in the political life of Nevada from the first decade of the 20th century through the early 1930s. Courtesy, Nevada Historical Society

Byington, 970; Stewart, 737. In some disbelief at the election results, the *Journal* returned to its theme that Roberts was too handicapped by his frontier ethics to win in a town that went to church as much as Reno did. The election pointed out the inaccuracy of this guess and illustrated the old political adage that the people usually did not vote the way they worshipped.

Who was Mayor E.E. Roberts? He was best known to Renoites as the popular and colorful mayor of Reno until his death in 1933. As Nevada's lone Congressman from 1911 to 1919, Roberts played the role of political maverick with a Republican label. He opposed President Wilson and his party's leadership when he voted against U.S. entrance into World War I in 1917, and he shunned the enthusiasm for reform in the Progressive era. Now, in his 2-½ terms as mayor he would rescue Reno from the clutches of the reformers.

The powerful Wingfield machine openly supported Roberts' reelection in 1927, as Roberts began acquiring the reputation as the permissive mayor of one of America's

Opposite, bottom: Edwin E. Roberts served as United States congressman from 1911 to 1918, and Reno's mayor from 1923 to 1933. Under Roberts' administration, Reno's divorce trade flourished, as well as prostitution and the illegal liquor business. Courtesy, Nevada Historical Society

Below: In 1927 the residency requirement for receiving a Nevada divorce was reduced to three months. Four years later, the Nevada Legislature established the present six-weeks residency. This rendering reflects a prevailing national view of Nevada and the divorce trade.

sauciest towns. Roberts made no secret of his contempt for Prohibition and winked at its lax enforcement in Reno. When he ran for his third term in 1931, the minister of the First Methodist Church invited him to speak from the pulpit. In that famous speech he advocated placing open barrels of whiskey on every street corner with ladles for all. The minister and the Methodists who were among the leading supporters of Prohibition were shocked. Shortly afterwards the Methodist Bishop transferred the minister from the Reno church.

By the end of the 1920s events relating to matrimony played an increasing role in Reno's economy. Local papers regularly carried the events of divorce trials that might involve misconduct or large settlements. In 1931 Reno divorce court judge George A. Bartlett's philosophic study of marriage and divorce appeared in Reno book stores as well as throughout the nation. Entitled *Men, Women and Conflict: An Intimate Study of Love, Marriage & Divorce*, it drew upon his many years of experience, and included advice to

young wives and husbands along with comments on birth control, adultery, children, and divorce law. The Nevada legislature in 1927 reduced the divorce residency requirement in Nevada from six months to three months. In 1931 the legislature made the residency period a mere six weeks. Nevada had been threatened with competition from other states like Arkansas and Idaho. None, however, dared to match Nevada's scandalous six-week law.

Another matrimony-related development was the passage by the California legislature of the so-called "three-day gin marriage law" in 1927. Californians became convinced that a waiting period before marriage would help prevent bad marriages. The absence of similar restrictions in Nevada spurred a marriage boom that offered good business to what would later be called "marryin' Sams" who flocked to Reno to perform ceremonies. They were precursors of the wedding chapels that dotted Reno streets in later years. The building of the new Victory Highway beginning in 1925 over the Sierra directly through the Truckee Canyon brought Reno

The automobile meant faster services for Reno, and the United States Mail was no exception. Courtesy, Nevada Historical Society

divorce and marriage much closer to California. By 1933 the number of marriages in Reno were nearly 2,000 more than the number of divorces. The usual number of divorces a year in the late 1920s and early 1930s was 2,500, but after the passage of the six-week law in 1931, there were 4,250—more than double the number in 1930. Reno put divorce within the financial reach of more people, helping to democratize a process that was once reserved for the famous and rich.

The famous and rich still flocked to the city, though. As the 1920s began many were from the new movie industry in Hollywood. "America's Sweetheart," Mary Pickford, showed up in Minden in 1920 with her Reno lawyer Pat McCarran to divorce Owen Moore in order to marry Douglas Fairbanks. The divorce was widely publicized and McCarran reputedly received (although this is seriously disputed) a $20,000 fee plus a home in Reno worth another $20,000.

The attraction of popular movie stars to Reno added to the glamor of the Reno Divorce Colony. And the stars who weren't there in person were there on film. Movies were becoming one of America's most popular leisure pastimes and the movie houses in Reno—the Wigwam, the Granada, the Majestic, the Reno, and Nevada theaters constantly advertised the appearance of movies with such stars as Gloria

Swanson, Sally O'Neil, and Ramon Navarro.

In addition to the revolution in entertainment, the 1920s brought a revolution in personal transportation. The automobile touched almost every aspect of American life from the way people earned their money to the ways they spent it. Remote cities like Reno had always relied upon the railroad as their lifeline to the outside world, but now the automobile opened other options. The public's insatiable demand for mass-produced, low-cost autos created new businesses in tire outlets, gasoline stations, auto parts stores, and a host of other industries. The new mode of transportation demanded better roads and even cross-country highways to which government was forced to respond at the local and national levels. A series of Good Road Acts beginning in 1916 committed the federal government to the building of interstate highways. This followed a largely private and local effort to build the transcontinental Lincoln Highway beginning in 1914 from New York City to San Francisco with an offshoot to Los Angeles. Across Nevada the Lincoln Highway took what would become the U.S. 50 route leaving Carson City as well as Reno important beneficiaries of the effort.

After the war the new federal highway across the state took a route along the Humboldt River, through Reno and then through the Truckee Canyon route to Sacramento. The new

Below: A shuttlebus for Reno's Golden Hotel is depicted here in about 1924. Located on Center Street, the Golden was one of Reno's leading hotels until it burned in 1962. Courtesy, Nevada Historical Society

Bottom: Assay offices became important businesses in Reno as the city served the constant prospecting in the mountains and deserts of Nevada. V.M. "Spike" Henderson is shown here in this assay office on North Sierra Street in 1922. Courtesy, Jean C. Hubbard

"Victory Highway" guaranteed that Reno would reap huge rewards from the advent of the automobile. To celebrate the ongoing work on the new Victory Highway (U.S. 40) and the final completion of the Lincoln Highway, Nevada and California sponsored the Transcontinental Highways Exposition from June 1 to August 1, 1927, in Reno. Idlewild Park became the site of the Exposition. Here the State of California built the California Building, offering it as a gift to the people of Nevada. The carnival atmosphere added to Idlewild's usual attractions: an animal park, a fish hatchery, and a public campground in addition to exhibits from many of the Western states. At the close of the Exposition the newspapers said that it helped travelers to discover that the "Great American Desert" could be easily reached and crossed by automobile, and further that it was not a desert at all, "but a vast region teeming with flourishing ranches, rich mining districts, and prosperous cities in a thriving American state." While the exposition did not draw the expected large crowds from throughout the nation, it did inform thousands of neighboring Californians that Reno was located just across the Sierra Nevada range, a few hours away. The full impact of this fact would not be felt until the 1950s and 1960s; the Depression and the war delayed it.

The airplane offered another link to the outside world with the building of Reno's first airfield in 1920 and the beginning of regularly scheduled passenger flights in 1927. The new radio station, owned by Sacramento interests, became Reno's first commercial radio station (KOH) in the same year. A more accessible Reno brought a marriage trade, a divorce trade, and finally the seekers of the illicit pleasures of gambling, drinking, and prostitution. Unquestionably the many years of office holding by Mayor Roberts helped to mark

Famed transatlantic aviator Charles A. Lindbergh visited Reno on September 19, 1927, on a national tour sponsored by the Guggenheim Aviation Fund. Courtesy, Nevada Historical Society

Bottom: Airmail service became a regular part of Reno life following the construction of Reno's first airfield in 1920. Shown here is the first flight out of Reno for the new mail service, September 11, 1920. Courtesy, Nevada Historical Society

Reno as an easy place to obtain almost anything money could buy without fear of the law. Figures from the underworld of the East and San Francisco saw Reno as a safe place to hide out, and even a profitable place to live. The extensive power of George Wingfield, now the owner of the new and modern Riverside Hotel, tended to foster lax law enforcement in areas of personal choice—drinking, gambling, prostitution, and divorce. Wingfield exerted tremendous political influence over the state from his offices (known as "the cave") on the second floor of the Reno National Bank. The law firm headed by William Woodburn and George Thatcher also operated from the cave, helping to direct state politics through something called a "Bi-partisan Machine." Wingfield was a power in the Republican Party and his lawyer associates controlled the Democratic Party. Not much escaped their attention in either Nevada or Reno politics. Their telephone number, 4111, became famous. It was a number that elected officials dialed before making appointments or casting votes in the legislature or even Congress.

Founded as Fogus' Mill in 1868, the Riverside Mill on East Second Street continues to be a landmark in the community. The present building dates from 1902 and is shown here in 1921. Courtesy, Nevada Historical Society

A cut below the Wingfield political machine were the operations of James McKay and William Graham in Reno. The two owned gambling dens, drinking parlors, and were behind the red-light district. The Stockade—or Crib, as it was called in the 1920s and 1930s—consisted of a series of small motel-like apartments, east of Lake Street and near the river. From these rooms prostitutes operated in eight-hour, around-the-clock shifts. Some said that profits from this enterprise reached into the highest levels of Reno society. In 1934 *Fortune* magazine referred to the five who ruled Reno. They included Wingfield, Woodburn, Thatcher, McKay, and Graham. McKay and Graham owned the Cal-Neva Lodge at North Lake Tahoe, the Willows Roadhouse west of Reno, and had investments in many other establishments, including the Reno Social Club, in partnership with Wingfield. Their businesses involved the risks of running liquor from the Bay Area across state lines. They occasionally harbored big-time criminals—Baby Face Nelson, Ma Barker, and perhaps Alvin Karpis—from the Midwest in their Reno dives and laundered money and securities received from outside connections.

The FBI finally brought charges that took them to trial in 1934. One of the chief witnesses against them was Roy Frisch, cashier of the Wingfield-owned Riverside Bank in Reno. Before Frisch could testify, he disappeared while on his way to a movie in Reno from his Court Street home. It was rumored that he was "rubbed out" by Baby Face Nelson as a favor to Graham and McKay for their protection in Reno. Possibly Frisch's body was tossed down a mine shaft near Yerington or sent to the bottom of Lake Tahoe in a cement casket. The event is one of Reno's unsolved crime mysteries and illustrates the sordid side of the fun and good times that Mayor Roberts helped protect in Reno.

The fall of the stock market in 1929 signaled the end of the "Roaring Twenties" for Reno and the nation. A drought in 1930-1931 dealt crippling blows to the stock and feed crop industries in the state. This meant a constantly higher debt structure for the state's ranchers and greater risk for the financial institutions that kept backing them. One of these financial institutions was the chain of 12 banks owned by Wingfield. By the summer of 1932 the banks were closed, including Reno's Riverside Bank, under a general statewide "bank holiday." But the Wingfield banks would never reopen: they were ordered into receivership in late 1933. The party was over for the Wingfield financial and political machine in the state. The Depression destroyed a banking empire that had shifted many of its investments into the uncertain future of Nevada agriculture and range stock industries.

Before the disastrous failure of the Wingfield banks, Nevada in 1931 startled the nation by re-legalizing gambling in the state. In the same year the legislature passed the six-week divorce residency law as Reno businessmen cheered it on. In the wake of these events another one of those famous Fourth of July boxing matches was scheduled. This match featured Max Baer and Paulino Uzcudun, "the bouncing Basque," who surprisingly defeated the future heavyweight champion. But despite the heady celebrations over legislation that made Reno wider open than ever, the decade began a serious time for Renoites. Easy divorce, legal gambling and legal prostitution, as well as the ready availability of drink, made Reno the target of national criticism.

A series of articles in *The Christian Century* magazine by Paul Hutchinson—entitled "Nevada—A Prostitute State," "Reno—A Wide-Open Town," "Reno's Divorce Mill," and "Can Reno Be Cured?"—portrayed Reno as the leading culprit in a statewide conspiracy to make money from sin. But the author warned that Nevada and Reno would ultimately reap the whirlwind with a disorganized and crime-ridden society shot through with the social problems of venereal disease, alcoholism, suicide, and juvenile delinquency. The International Society of Christian Endeavor (Protestant youth) asserted, "Reno is a blot on civilization, a menace to the American home and national prestige."

But Reno had more to worry about than the consequences of sin, which it had already accepted as a fact of everyday life by 1931. The new legal gambling had little impact on the Depression-struck economy. Flashy gambling palaces did not all of a sudden spring up along Virginia Street after legaliza-

Douglas Alley, the busiest little street in the busiest little city, is shown here in 1931. Along each side of the street people entered any doorway and found themselves in gambling establishments where they sought to woo "Lady Luck." Courtesy, National Archives, Washington, D.C.

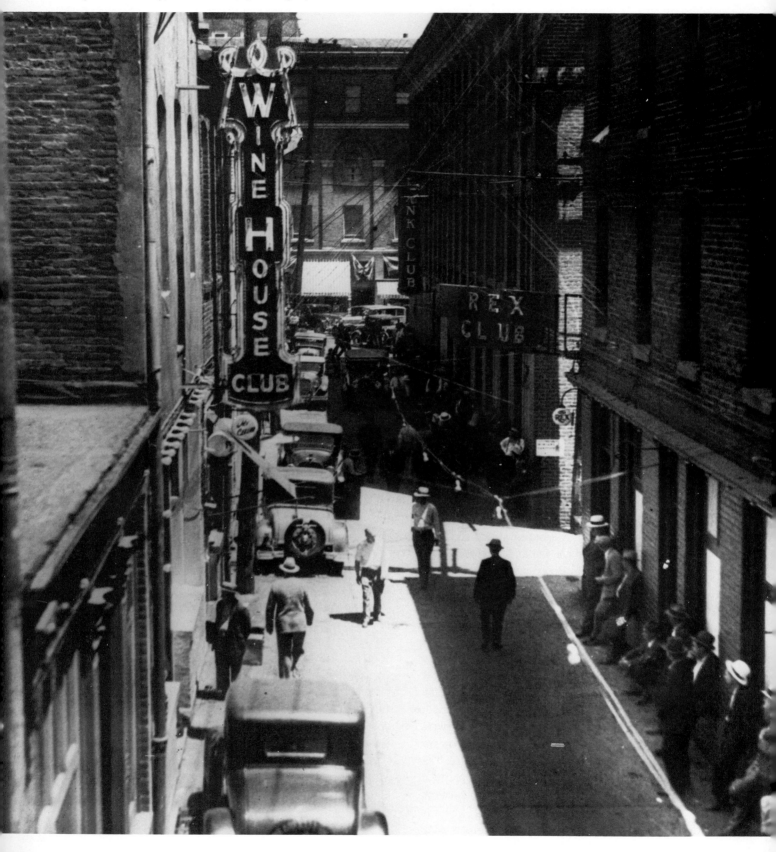

tion. Gambling houses still retained a secretive air, preferring to remain in the back alleys—especially Douglas Alley, where the Bank Club, the Rex Club, and the Wine House Club did business. Inside these clubs the atmosphere was dark and dingy. Older, bald-headed men with green eyeshades usually presided over smoke-engulfed gaming tables. There were no glamorous floor shows or cocktail waitresses serving drinks. The gambling dens served a cheerless male gambling clientele. Legalized gambling continued to assume a low profile which reflected the fear that if it drew too much attention to itself, the anti-gambling forces would once again outlaw gambling. Graham and McKay continued their activities, although Graham displayed a violent streak when he shot a man in Douglas Alley. Graham pled self-defense and a grand jury quickly dismissed murder charges. Eventually the federal government succeeded in jailing these two shady Reno figures. The divorce business had problems during the decade, with Las Vegas commanding attention when Clark Gable obtained the divorce he needed in order to marry Carole Lombard in that new southern Nevada city that had sprung to life after the building of Boulder Dam.

As the stillness of the Depression settled on Reno hope faded that gambling and divorce would make the city Depression-proof. With the failure of the Wingfield banks, the political machine that had ruled Nevada for nearly two decades also toppled. The new political currents swept Renoite Pat McCarran, the longtime enemy of Wingfield, into the U.S. Senate. The Democratic Party captured offices in the state and brought Franklin D. Roosevelt to the Presidency in the fall of 1932. The programs of the Roosevelt Administration—the CWA, PWA, CCC, WPA, among others—had a tremendous impact on communities throughout America and Reno was no exception. Reno projects included building the Mackay Stadium at the University of Nevada, building

Below: A Works Progress Administration crew is shown here laying a pipeline to the new Reno Municipal Golf Course in the late 1930s. Courtesy, National Archives, Washington, D.C.

Bottom: Works Progress Administration funds not only aided the unemployed, but also established nursery schools in Reno during hard times. Courtesy, National Archives, Washington, D.C.

school and park playgrounds, clearing irrigation ditches, constructing Virginia Lake Park, and building ski runs and lodges in the mountains above the city.

As the old Wingfield bipartisan machine crumbled, it was replaced by New Deal politicians and their local captains in the Democratic Party, who controlled the distribution of relief and employment. Unlike many industrial cities Reno did not face immediate devastating unemployment from the Depression. While the economy was slow many joined in the make-work and community-improvement programs that provided jobs. An important contribution of the programs to the city was relief for the hundreds of transients who streamed in and out of town. Many were on their way to California, or coming back disappointed. The Transient Service established camps to house people in hastily built quarters, encouraged garden planting, and brought logs into wood lots so transients could cut their own fuel wood.

A milestone in New Deal community achievements in the city was the building of a new Idlewild swimming pool in 1937. PWA funds provided half of the $70,000 price tag for the pool while Reno came up with the rest in a special bond issue. On hand at the dedication ceremonies on June 17, 1937 was Senator McCarran. In his speech to the crowd he pointed out the special advantages that American youth enjoyed over the youth of foreign countries whose governments, he said,

were weak and disrupted by war. He reminded the Reno audience that America held the balance of power for world peace and it was important that its government remain a showcase for democracy. McCarran spoke these words about seemingly far-away problems while children impatiently

Laughton's (Lawton's) Hot Springs, located west of Reno on the old Lincoln Highway, is shown here in the early 1930s. Founded in the 1880s, the resort attracted locals, tourists, and, later, divorcés. Max Baer, later to become World Heavyweight Champion, trained at the resort in 1931. Courtesy, Nevada Historical Society

awaited their first plunge into the cold, unheated waters of the new pool.

While Reno took New Deal aid and as much as was offered, it did not feel overly indebted to the generosity of federal programs. It enjoyed gambling license fees and tax revenues which at the time went almost exclusively to county and city governments. Although few would admit it, Reno had already made its choice for profits and legalized vices. It seemed fairly self-satisfied even in the grip of the Depression. This aspect of self-content helps explain why the outlook of the New Deal never took firm root in the private-enterprise soil of Reno. While other states launched their own "little New Deals" which offered increased public services and heavier taxation, Nevada shunned such state programs.

Under the promptings of northern Nevadan Norman Biltz, who advocated the economics of "One Sound State," Nevada emerged from the Depression a lightly taxed state. Biltz, a real estate promoter at Tahoe and of Nevada ranch lands, in the depths of the Depression determined to sell Nevada land on the basis of a favorable tax structure for the wealthy in the state. When other states moved to expand their governmental services in the spirit of the New Deal and sought new sources of wealth to tax, Biltz worked for limitations on taxes in Nevada. Constitutional prohibitions on inheritance and estate taxes and a limitation on state property tax rates were all in effect by 1942. This made Nevada and Reno attractive for the rich as they fled "soak the rich" taxes in other states. Biltz, soon to be known as the "Duke of Nevada," quickly impressed upon them the wisdom of buying large tracts of Nevada real estate to legitimatize their residency. For Nevada's less well-to-do, the "One Sound State" might also mean lower taxes, but it offered few services in education, health care, recreation, and pension systems.

While Reno continued to welcome the divorce crowd and the wealthy seeking refuge from punitive tax laws in other states, its doors opened to a new class of gambling entrepreneur. These new gamblers ultimately transformed Reno gambling houses, removing them from the alleys along Commercial Row, and placing them under bright lights in prominent locations on Virginia Street. Harold Smith arrived in 1936 and soon after his father, Raymond I. "Pappy" Smith, and his brother Raymond. They established a small gambling club on Virginia Street. One of the early attractions of Harolds Club was a roulette game played with white mice. William Harrah, after earlier unsuccessful attempts beginning in 1937, opened the Tango Club in Douglas Alley in 1939 and eventually expanded into Virginia Street. Both of these clubs were destined to revolutionize Reno gambling; but it would take the upheaval of World War II and the resulting social changes in American society to help bring this about.

CHAPTER FIVE

RENO AND THE OUTSIDE WORLD

On the eve of World War II Reno stood on the threshold of two of its most expansive decades. The town was still the first major stop on a transcontinental railroad after leaving Sacramento and crossing the Sierra. The steam trains, with their mournful whistles, plied their ways east and west across the Truckee Meadows as they had done ever since 1868. But the steam trains would give way to the diesel, then to the automobile and airplane. They would all bring Reno vastly closer to the country's main population centers.

A part of Reno had always been very much in touch with the world outside, thanks to the divorce industry, the marriage trade, and various New Deal programs. But now there was something new to bring the outside world to Reno: gambling.

The search for a wider gambling market coincided with the beginning of war. Harolds Club launched a nationwide advertising campaign to lure tourists to Reno—not explicitly to gamble, but rather to have fun. Under the promptings of Raymond I. "Pappy" Smith, the club opened with wide windows on its Virginia Street entrance and neon lights inviting all to come in. Many old-time Reno gamblers feared that Harolds Club's publicity would again provoke a reaction by the community to restrict gambling. Instead Harolds took the initiative of placing "Harolds Club or Bust" signs throughout the nation, advertising the good times to be had in Reno. Harolds Club lowered minimum bets at the poker and 21 tables to 10 cents, introduced penny roulette at a time when 25 cents was the lowest at other houses, and featured 5- and 10-cent slots. To create a broader and more middle-class clientele for gambling, Harolds also made the club more attractive and advertised along the roadsides and on a new medium, radio. The message brought thousands of customers to Reno with high hopes and expectations of good, clean fun. Women came into the club to gamble and observe, as did many others who would never have entered the darker hovels along Douglas Alley. Harolds Club changed the image of

Reno gambling from a low-life pursuit to an exciting, normal everyday leisure-time activity. This was a remarkable feat which was accomplished in a very short period of time.

With the influx of California tourists, longtime Nevada watchers saw Reno playing a major role in recapturing wealth that the world had taken from Nevada during the brief boom years of the Comstock. The war no doubt aided the process. As the Southwestern states became important training areas for aerial war, soldiers were stationed at Nevada bases and the new army camp north of Reno was soon converted into an army air force base in 1942. Thousands of servicemen passed through Reno on their way to California destinations, witnessing firsthand the open and legal gambling in the city.

Even before Pearl Harbor, preparations for war were well underway. The nation had its first peacetime draft and new appropriations for military hardware were starting the nation's factories back to work and signaling the end of the Depression. Senator McCarran, who previously stood fast against American involvement in foreign wars, declared total commitment to war after the Japanese attack.

The war mobilization immediately restricted gasoline supplies and the use of automobiles. It also drew millions of men into the armed services and left the domestic work force starved for workers. Many wondered about the catastrophic effects upon the Reno tourist economy. But in the long run the war brought not catastrophe but a boom to the economy.

In Reno one result of the war was an increasing number of women dealers. They became Reno's equivalent to Rosie the Riveter in the shipyards. Unmistakably the hiring of women dealers promoted the new openness of Reno gambling, and what some called a democratization in the industry that Harolds Club had begun. Democratization of gambling did not include broaching the color line, however. Many clubs continued to carry "Colored Trade Not Solicited" signs well into the 1950s.

Even before the war, Nevada gambling clubs learned to

This mural above the entrance to Harolds Club celebrated the pioneer spirit of "those who blazed the trail." It offered tourists a familiar Western panorama as many enjoyed the new experience of free and open gambling along Reno's Virginia Street in the 1950s. Courtesy, Nevada Historical Society

augment gambling with entertainment packages which included top-name entertainment figures, inexpensive hotel accommodations, and good food and liquor at reasonable prices. This was the magic formula for attracting crowds to Reno. While the war postponed the advent of the civilian weekend tourist trade, the trade of military personnel was significant. The Reno Army Air Force Base (the name was changed to Stead Air Force Base in 1951) and the Naval Air Station at Fallon established a strong military presence in northern Nevada. All of the attractions of Reno made it a favorite liberty town for military personnel in Nevada and northern California.

But one traditional part of Reno would not survive the war. The federal government demanded, as it had during World War I, that houses of prostitution near military bases be closed. In 1942 a long-standing Reno tradition came to an end when city government closed down the prostitution section. The war and pressure from the government succeeded in doing what successive reform movements had failed to do in Reno. Mayor Harry E. Stewart, who was defeated on this issue in 1923, had the satisfaction of seeing the "cribs" closed when he again became Reno's mayor during the war. After the war, prostitution attempted to reestablish itself, but Washoe County declared it a public nuisance. Nevada courts upheld the authority of the county to regulate for the health, welfare, and morals of the people in a famous case, *Washoe County* v. *Cunningham* in 1949. Even the business community was content with the new situation, since the presence of

Below: Walter Van Tilburg Clark grew up in Reno and became the community's most famous literary figure. Courtesy, Nevada Historical Society

Bottom: Raymond I. "Pappy" Smith was the sparkplug of the Smith family's Harolds Club. Courtesy, Nevada Historical Society

legal prostitution would have sullied the image that the new breed of gamblers was trying to affix to Reno—a town with good, clean gambling fun.

Although the red-light district died with the war, gambling in downtown Reno began to dominate the center of the city during the 1940s. Walter Van Tilburg Clark called this "the treeless center of the city" in his long, elaborate novel on Reno, *The City of Trembling Leaves* (1945). He asserted that by this decade two Renos had emerged. The first was the Reno of tourists—the world of the croupier, the green felt jungle, or the "ersatz jungle," as Clark termed it. The "other" city was the Reno of green trees, bright sunlight, and majestic mountains. It was this second Reno that commanded the interest of novelist Clark, whose father presided over the University of Nevada from 1918 to 1938.

By the end of the war it was definitely the Reno of the downtown that attracted the attention of the world through advertisements and the tales told by returning military personnel. With the apparent success of the Reno economy even in the stress of wartime, the Mapes family, which had long been associated with Reno and the promotion of the rodeo, announced in 1947 plans for a new multi-story high-rise hotel in Reno to be built on the sight of the old post office building. This expression of faith in Reno came at a time when the postwar economy was slow and uncertain.

Others followed the Mapes' lead including some gamblers from the crime underworld of the East, who saw opportunity for legalized gambling businesses in Nevada. Lincoln

Below: Nevada's powerful Senator Pat McCarran made Reno his home base as he handled important senatorial assignments during and after World War II. Courtesy, Nevada Historical Society

Bottom: Reno casinos were the first in the state to employ female blackjack, or 21, dealers. The labor shortage during World War II offered women increased opportunities as casino dealers. Courtesy, Greater Reno-Sparks Chamber of Commerce

Below and opposite: The Mapes family (below, left to right), George, Charles, Jr., and Charles, were long associated with ranching and banking. Charles W. Mapes, his mother Gladys (opposite), and sister Gloria built the first multi-story hotel in postwar Reno in 1947. Courtesy, Nevada Historical Society

Below and opposite: The Mapes family (below, left to right), George, Charles, Jr., and Charles, were long associated with ranching and banking. Charles W. Mapes, his mother Gladys (opposite), and sister Gloria built the first multi-story hotel in postwar Reno in 1947. Courtesy, Nevada Historical Society

Fitzgerald, a onetime figure with the Detroit mob, became a co-owner of the Nevada Club. But it was to the new boomtown atmosphere of Las Vegas that a greater number of crime figures migrated including Benjamin "Bugsy" Siegel, who built the Flamingo Hotel there in 1946. Siegel was killed the following year in an apparent gangland slaying related to his business venture into Las Vegas gambling. Fitzgerald himself was attacked in a similar manner in Reno in 1949. But he survived his severe wounds to live a guarded life in Reno and eventually build Fitzgerald's Casino. The presence of organized crime in Nevada's two largest cities prompted investigations. The U.S. Senate's Select Committee on Crime came to Nevada in 1950 and captured national headlines by exposing the infiltration of crime figures into Nevada gambling. The response by state government to regulate gambling made the process of obtaining licenses more difficult, but did not make the restrictions retroactive.

Although the underworld became an acknowledged force in the growth of postwar Las Vegas and, to a lesser extent, in Reno, local government in Reno was more interested in questions of where gaming houses should be permitted to operate. In January of 1947 the City Council adopted a master plan for the city that restricted casino gambling to a commercial district along Virginia Street in the downtown. Eventually a "red line" was drawn around this district and the restriction was referred to for many years as Reno's Red Line Ordinance. It blocked the haphazard spread of casinos throughout the city.

Some critics said that the rule stifled growth and forced the city to fall behind Las Vegas; but the dynamic growth of Southern California and the access to inexpensive power from Boulder Dam (Hoover Dam after 1947) to power air conditioners probably were the key to Las Vegas' ability to surpass Reno.

In the same year that the Council drew a red-line boundary around gambling, Reno adopted the city-manager form of local government. Since the Progressive era, the city-manager structure of municipal government had been recognized as an important reform measure designed to bring efficient business methods to local government. Still, the reform of 1947 did not achieve a city-manager office that was above the politics surrounding the mayor and the council. Ideally the mayor and the council under this type of local government set the policies and the city manager administered the various departments of city government without council interference. This situation did not prevail until the early 1960s, when the city obtained a change in its charter to permit the greater independence of the manager and required candidates for the position to meet higher qualifications.

Restructuring local government accompanied readjustments in the local economy during the postwar period. Gambling, of course, was not the only business in town that aspired to growth. The development of ski resorts in nearby mountains boosted the slow winter economy. Among the other businessmen seeking opportunities was Edwin Bender, a member of an old Reno family that had pioneered business and banking in the city. During the war Bender became involved in warehousing goods for the federal government in Reno. Now he hoped this same business could continue in peacetime, for private industry.

Bender set in motion a campaign in the state legislature to have goods stored in the state, but since they would be scheduled for reshipment out of state, they would be exempt from state inventory taxes. The "free port" law passed the Nevada legislature in 1949 and eventually found its way into the Nevada state constitution in 1960. The 1949 law laid the foundation for a thriving Reno warehousing industry, offering employment and building contracts. And it was pollution-free, except for the exhaust from additional trucks which increasingly supplanted rail transport.

As Reno participated in the creation of new service industries catering to out-of-state customers—gambling, hotels, food services, warehousing, and winter sports—new residents flowed into the city. In the wartime and postwar periods Reno's population increased from 21,317 in 1940 to 32,497 in 1950, and to 51,470 in 1960. This represented a

dramatic increase in Reno's population in a matter of 20 years, and the end of growth was nowhere in sight.

As always with the influx of a new labor force into the state, questions relating to labor policy and the organization of labor arose, especially in the important food and drink industry. Reno had never been the site of a major struggle between labor and management that affected the entire state. But in the summer of 1949 Reno became the scene of a struggle by organized labor to unionize the bartending and culinary workers of the city. The confrontation had far-reaching effects on the statewide laws governing the relationship of labor and management.

Reno on the Fourth of July meant "rodeo" for almost three decades. The war years briefly cancelled the celebration but by 1948 and 1949 the festivities were more popular than ever. This was Reno's big money-making weekend of the summer. When William Royalty of the Bartenders and Culinary Union announced that picket lines would be set up outside many of the clubs and restaurants during the Independence Day weekend of 1949, shock spread throughout Reno. With negotiations underway since April, labor now chose the lucrative Fourth of July weekend to demand a full acceptance

of its demands for union recognition, pay raises, and equal pay for men and women waiters. Reno Mayor Francis "Tank" Smith appealed to labor to declare a truce until July 6. But Royalty replied that labor must use the rodeo weekend as a lever to achieve its goals. As soon as the union's plan became clear, the newspapers announced in full-page ads the formation of a Citizens' Emergency Committee, chaired by Forest Lovelock.

The committee issued a call to the people of Reno declaring: "Our vital tourist industry is threatened—you are now asked to help save it in this grave emergency." It explained that since April, negotiations had been underway between the union and hotels to organize their service workers (housekeepers, maids, bellhops, and elevator operators). Now, in order to save Reno's tourist industry over this important weekend, it called upon the public-spirited citizens of Reno "to roll up their sleeves and pitch in as dish washers, cooks helpers, waiters, bartenders, busboys, and any number of similar jobs." The plan was to serve meals to tourists in Powning and Horseman's parks so that no one would go away from Reno either hungry or disappointed by the lack of service. The committee disclaimed bias in the dispute and said the people taking part in the community effort should favor neither labor nor management. It was merely trying "to avert the grave threat to Reno's economic life."

The strike, originally scheduled for July 2, was postponed because of continuing negotiations until Sunday, July 3, at 2 p.m. Then an estimated 700 members of the Bartenders and Culinary Workers Union went on strike. A principal sticking point was the issue of equal pay for waiters and waitresses. Local newspapers became irate and accused union leader William Royalty, "who hasn't been here very long" of fashioning "a bludgeon out of the holiday conditions here to enforce his demands." They branded Royalty an "outside agitator"; union spokesmen replied that Royalty had been a resident of Reno since 1937 and certainly was not an outsider sent to Reno to stir up labor trouble.

The confrontation over the Fourth of July Weekend left fear and resentment on both sides. Labor resented the spontaneous community support for what it interpreted as the intransigent and anti-union attitude of the clubs. Management and community leaders nursed a resentment and a fear of the power of labor in the community and the possibility that labor would demand a greater share in the decision-making processes of the tourist and gaming industry, Reno's lifeblood.

The Fourth of July incident eventually ignited a spark that pushed Reno and Nevada into the mainstream of the postwar reaction against the power that labor had gained during the

New Deal and the war. Early in the dispute, the newspapers took a larger view of the labor-management confrontation in Reno. They said that the current trouble was an example of irresponsible labor leadership of the kind that helped keep the recently passed Taft-Hartley Act (which was an attempt to correct what were seen as union abuses) on the federal law books. The most offensive part of the act for organized labor was Section 14 (b), which gave states the right to prohibit entirely the requirement of union membership as a condition of employment. This section opened the door for many states to place restrictions upon union organization through the enactment of so-called "right-to-work laws." During the 1950s the battle over the passage of "right-to-work laws" dominated the political struggles in many states. The crisis in Reno led directly in the next session of the legislature in 1951

to the passage of a right-to-work law subject to the approval of the voters in the 1952 election. Voters of the state approved it by a narrow margin of over 1,000 votes in the same year that Dwight D. Eisenhower was elected as the first Republican President in 20 years.

After the election Nevada took its place along with many other states in the Southwest, Midwest, and of course the South, as a right-to-work state. During the entire battle, right-to-work advocates pointed to Reno as an example of a city and an industry that could be held hostage by the unlimited power of organized "labor gangsters." The incidents in Reno on that Fourth of July weekend convinced many Nevadans that labor should be restrained.

The 1950s for Reno was a decade that saw the successful growth of its tourism and gaming economy along with other diversified industries in the Truckee Meadows. Some were disappointed that Reno did not transform itself into a glittering showcase similar to Las Vegas. The cow-town, honky-tonk atmosphere persisted in the downtown as Reno was slow to build convention and auditorium facilities that could serve national conventions. Perhaps the fact that Reno did have a diversified economy drawing upon warehousing, some light industry, the military (from the stimulus of the Korean War), and surrounding agriculture lessened the single-minded purpose of Renoites to compete with Las Vegas. But the downtown community never lost sight for a minute of the importance of the outside world's tourist trade to the economy of Reno.

Rodeo had always been a chief drawing card over the years. The traditional dates on the Fourth of July weekend were reserved for the rodeo, but some now argued that the rodeo dates should be moved away from the Fourth weekend to provide two big weekends for Reno instead of just one. The rodeo dates were changed to mid-June in 1960, leaving the Fourth weekend open for the traditional Independence Day tourist holiday in Reno. The prominence of the Reno rodeo on the nationwide circuit suffered, but Reno now looked to additional tourist dollars. Harolds Club owner "Pappy" Smith continued the struggle to make Reno more accessible to the world when he launched a campaign for the building of a four-lane highway over the Sierra. Nevada Congressmen soon heard the appeals from their Reno constituents to support appropriations for interstate highway acts. Renoites and Northern Californians along U.S. 40 became particularly concerned after Harolds Club publicity people spoke to chambers of commerce and placed signs along the route saying, "Let's make this four lane. Write your Congressman." With the passage of the National Defense Highway

Opposite, bottom: The old Virginia and Truckee Railroad bridge across the Truckee finally met its end during a flood in 1955. The V&T ceased service in 1950 after many unprofitable years. Courtesy, Nevada Historical Society

Below: This photograph features the finish line for the ski races at the 1960 Winter Olympics held at Squaw Valley, California, 45 minutes from Reno. Courtesy, Nevada Historical Society

Act of 1956, money became available for the project when the government commenced a nationwide highway program.

Much of the new modern four-lane highway across the Sierra was completed when the world literally did come to Reno in February 1960 for the 1960 Winter Olympics held at Squaw Valley, California, just 50 miles west of Reno. The event also brought home to Renoites the importance of airline transportation to its tourist trade.

While Reno looked to the outside world for its dollars, it faced internal troubles in the decade. Water—too much or too little of it—often became an issue. One problem was that Reno faced floods from the usually delightful Truckee River in 1950, 1952, and 1955. The Army Corps of Engineers responded to the challenge of flood control on the river by building additional reservoirs in the mountains, especially Stampede Dam on the Little Truckee and Prosser Reservoir. But the shortage of water for the city's growth probably was a greater problem in the long run. Some suggested Reno's situation required water meters in the city and county; others declared that Reno's green lawns and trees would perish if citizens were forced to pay higher prices for metered water.

Reno city government toward the end of the 1950s was,

unfortunately, ill-equipped to deal with the city's problems, demonstrating immaturity and inefficiency. The reforms promised by the city-manager style of municipal government seemed to be producing few good results. Mayor Bud Baker and his council (1959-1963), according to local newspapers, made "a circus" out of local government and failed to move ahead quickly on plans for a convention center and a local performing-arts building. It became increasingly clear to all that Reno desperately needed an intelligent city government to facilitate its multi-million dollar tourist trade and to act as a public partner in the enterprise. This became the challenge of the next decades as Reno tied itself ever more closely to the national tourist economy.

To the outsider, Reno's glaring peculiarity was not divorce, as in bygone days, but the new gaming empires. Harolds Club stood as a monument to its success, and others shared in that success. Harrah's, for instance, opened a new, splashy club at South Lake Tahoe in 1955. No more could gaming remain an inconspicuous part of the city's life: now it was Reno's dominant economic force, for better or worse. Years before Reno had made its decision on this question, and now many wondered if it did not have a tiger by the tail.

CHAPTER SIX

RENO: THE BIGGEST LITTLE CITY

When Reno was young it boasted extravagantly of its future as the new Denver of the intermountain west. By the 1920s Reno businessmen felt the necessity for the spice of naughtiness to keep the local economy fit and growing. As the century moved into its final quarter Reno stood in the midst of a bonanza growth period. The new enterprises brought huge amounts of outside investment dollars, creating new casinos and hotels that sprouted from the downtown streets like cheat grass on the Nevada ranges after a spring rain.

Beyond the downtown streets and east toward Sparks, the rise of the gigantic MGM Grand Hotel and Casino gradually took shape in 1977 despite earlier prohibitions against the spread of gambling from the downtown area. Reno began to sell itself not just as a tourist mecca with gambling, skiing, and sunshine, but also as a site for new light industry that could diversify the economy. But in the midst of its attempt to attract both new gambling and work-a-day industry, Reno city government faced the task of keeping its own house in order.

Reno city government in the beginning of the 1960s undertook capital improvements in convention facilities, auditoriums, a new city hall, and the expansion of public safety services. Faced with the expenditure of millions of dollars, Reno city government unfortunately lacked public confidence to carry out these large tasks. Leading members of the community responded by forming a citizens' committee to reform the city charter. Headed by longtime Reno educator and former superintendent of Washoe County Schools Earl Wooster, the committee formed in 1961 because the present city government "left something to be desired," according to Wooster. In the 1961 legislative session the committee became a driving force behind a measure to alter the city charter. The new charter proposal, which had to first, according to Nevada law, obtain the approval of the legislature before it went to city voters, discarded the ward system of council representation making way for elections at large. It also abol-

ished the elected mayor and established a stronger city manager. With the legislature's approval, Reno stood on the verge of obtaining a true city-manager form of municipal government comparable to the model municipal government that had been proposed during the Progressive era at the beginning of the century.

Reno newspapers supported the charter change, pointing out in the manner of earlier Progressive reformers that the ward system of representation led to "ward heeling and other ills." In the proposed charter, ward boundaries would be revised but generally retained. Candidates for five of the seven council positions would be required to live within the wards they represented, but all of the voters of the city would vote on them. Two at-large council members would be elected with no restrictions upon where they lived in the city. After elections the council would elect a figurehead mayor from amongst themselves. The mayor would preside at council meetings and represent the city on ceremonial occasions.

With the support of newspapers and an active campaign by the League of Women Voters, Reno accepted in November of 1962 the charter changes. The favorable vote pointed attention to city elections in 1963. Again, Wooster led a committee. This time it was called the Committee of Fifty. It met regularly at the El Cortez Hotel and dedicated itself to the election of a new and qualified council under the new charter. The committee solicited money, persuaded respected personalities to seek election, and promised them financial support in the campaign. The committee decided to shun support from gambling houses despite their central economic role suggesting the continuing failure of the clubs to be accepted as first-class business citizens. By the 1980s, however, candidates for office in Reno municipal elections were no longer reluctant to accept contributions from major casinos. Clearly in the intervening 20 years gambling houses had gained full-fledged acceptance into Reno life and politics.

The newly elected council members, all of whom had the

In 1964 leading downtown casinos stepped forward to purchase a new arch to replace the older model. The Reno Arch and its famous slogan have been trademarks of the city since the late 1920s. Courtesy, Greater Reno-Sparks Chamber of Commerce

Local architect Hewitt C. Wells created a park in the library when he designed the central branch of the Washoe County Library in Reno. Courtesy, Greater Reno-Sparks Chamber of Commerce

blessings of the reform committee, included Roy Bankofier, John Chism, William Gravelle, Claude Hunter, Hugo Quilici, Ed Spoon, and Clarence Thornton. As provided by the charter, the council chose the mayor from its own group. Hugo Quilici was the first mayor under the new charter that gave Reno a true city-manager type of municipal government. The city manager, Joe Latimore, had come to Reno in 1960 to help bail out the previous council from some of its troubles. His popularity in the city assured him a continued appointment until his retirement in 1974. By that time, he said, "things were starting to get away" from him. His administrative methods, said one Reno newspaper, no longer suited the "new" Reno of the mid-1970s, a city that had outgrown his style of close personal interaction.

During these years, despite the turmoil at city hall, local government moved toward the completion of significant public buildings. The Washoe County Public Library (1966) designed by local architect Hewitt C. Wells became an impressive addition to downtown Reno through the aid of the

Max C. Fleischmann Foundation. The attractive Fleischmann Planetarium took shape on the campus of the University of Nevada in 1963. Harrah's opened its world-famous auto collection in 1962. The dome-shaped Pioneer Theater and Auditorium occupied a choice site on Virginia Street within easy walking distance of major hotels and casinos. The decision was made to locate the Centennial Coliseum, a larger convention facility, south on Virginia Street outside of the downtown. While this drew much criticism, it was argued that many out-of-town groups seeking convention sites would desire to be somewhat removed from the downtown gambling scene. By 1965 a new city hall, jail, and municipal court building added to the presence and vitality of local government.

Both Reno and Sparks demonstrated their determination to be independent governmental entities when voters in 1967 rejected a proposal to merge the two city governments. Suggestions for merging local governments also included combining city and county governments. Underlying these moves

Opened to the public in 1962, Harrah's Auto Collection grew out of the personal collection of William Harrah, and has proved to be an enduring attraction. Courtesy, Harrah's

were recommendations by local planners, including Reno city manager Latimore, that the Truckee Meadows should embrace a regional planning concept to prepare for future growth. This led to the appointment of several Blue Ribbon Committees that made reports and recommendations on the directions and possibilities of growth in the area through the year 2000. The predictions suggested unprecedented growth and the necessity for immediate planning to guide the de-

velopment. At stake was the protection of the quality of life in the Truckee Meadows and the wise use of scarce resources, especially water.

While Reno officialdom tried to polish up the image of Reno city government, prominent casinos stepped forward to support one of Reno's longstanding trademarks. The world-famous arch proclaiming Reno "The Biggest Little City in the World" stood in need of replacement by 1962. In

Below: The Nobel Getchell Library on the University of Nevada-Reno campus separates the modern section from the older ivy-covered buildings. Courtesy, Greater Reno-Sparks Chamber of Commerce

the following year, six downtown casinos (Harolds Club, the Nevada Club, Horseshoe Club, Primadonna, Colony Club, and Poor Pete's) donated $100,000 to replace the old arch. This happened in 1964 and the new arch was deeded to the city in 1969. The old arch found a home in one of the city's new parks, Paradise Park, on the way to Sparks near Oddie Boulevard.

Beyond the glitter of the downtown's bright lights, Reno's artistic and cultural community began a revival in these years of sustained prosperity. Supported to a great extent by a growing university community, theater, music, visual arts, and opera made increasing appearances on the Reno scene. Since 1935 the Reno Little Theater never missed a season and enjoyed large audiences during Reno's growth after 1960. The community's musical life always drew upon the large number of performing musicians associated with entertainment in Reno as well as the university's music department. The Reno Municipal Band under the direction of N.A. "Tink" Tinkham provided popular summertime-in-the-park entertainment for 31 years. The Community Concert series began as early as 1935 and celebrated its 25th anniversary in 1960. Its offerings were augmented by the Public Occasions Board at the University of Nevada. In 1969 musical devotees supported the founding of the Reno Philharmonic Orchestra under the direction of Gregory Stone. In 1977 the Nevada Symphony Orchestra made its appearance in the Truckee Meadows. The work of the Nevada Art League during the 1960s eventually led to the formation of the Sierra Arts Foundation.

Early in the history of the West and the Washoe Country, opera made its appearance. Piper's Opera House and Maguire's Opera House in Virginia City during the Comstock era, Dyer's Theater in Reno (1871), and the McKissick Theater (1887) provided facilities for performances before enthusiastic Western audiences. In 1967 the Nevada Opera Guild began. Under the direction of Theodore Puffer, who specialized in translating productions into English, the Nevada Opera Guild attracted nationwide attention by 1974. By the early 1970s a common bumper sticker on Reno automobiles read, "Reno Loves Opera." Finally, the Young Audiences Program helped bring the appreciation of classical music to schoolchildren.

More bizarre elements also marked the Reno scene in these years. When prostitution was banned from Washoe County,

Opposite, bottom: The controversial and futuristic Pioneer Theater Auditorium across the street from the Washoe County Court House was completed in 1967. Courtesy, Greater Reno-Sparks Chamber of Commerce

Below: The warehousing industry dominates the Reno-Sparks industrial area, highlighting the success of Nevada's "freeport law," and Reno's central location as a redistribution point for Western markets. Courtesy, Greater Reno-Sparks Chamber of Commerce

operations promptly shifted to counties east of Reno where laws regarding prostitution were matters of local city and county option. One establishment near the highway east of Reno and Sparks was the Mustang Ranch under the ownership of Joe and Sally Conforte. Joe Conforte became a wealthy, controversial figure in the Reno-Sparks area. He occasionally donated money to worthy causes, which usually produced differences of opinion as to whether the money should be accepted or not. Usually it was accepted. But when Conforte offered to bankroll a public transportation system in the form of urban bus service, local government refused after some heated debate. Not until 1978 would Reno-Sparks have a well-financed and extensive public transportation system.

Another socially controversial event that started in Reno in 1976 was the annual Gay Rodeo, attracting thousands of gay men from throughout the country, especially from San Francisco. Renoites, with their traditional "live-and-let-live" attitude raised few objections, though this event did strain that attitude.

Diversity in the arts and life-styles also accompanied new diversity in industry for Reno. In 1968 inventor/industrialist William Lear brought Lear Industries to Reno, establishing it on 3,500 acres of the abandoned Stead Air Force Base which he bought from the city and converted into an industrial park. The closure of the base north of the city in 1966 had been an economic shock, causing thousands to leave Reno and a drop

of $34 million in retail sales during the first year. The arrival of the company and the announcement by Lear that his new project would attempt to develop an economical steam car stirred the imagination of the Reno business community. The vision of Reno as a site for new light industry seemed about to be realized. Lear embodied the ideal which many Renoites cherished—that practical, down-to-earth industry could consider Reno as a development site.

Lear's experiments with a steam engine were particularly timely during the years when gasoline prices skyrocketed because of the Arab oil embargo, but the results proved unmarketable. Nevertheless after the Lear investments came the announcement by the JC Penney Company in the mid-1970s that it would build one of its largest warehouses north of the city near the Lear facility. Upon its completion in 1979 after 26 months of construction, the $50-million warehouse, which covered over 36 acres, employed at times 2,000 people whose combined annual earnings were $12 million. Both industries were major economic breakthroughs for Reno, helping the city to diversify its economic base.

On the state level during the late 1960s, Governor Paul Laxalt moved to change state gaming laws to permit out-of-state corporations to enter the Nevada gambling business. At the time it was widely acknowledged that these moves were designed to accommodate Howard Hughes and bring "respectable" Hughes money into Nevada gambling. New

Below: Reno's annual rodeo remains one of the city's biggest attractions, drawing fans and residents to its exciting Western festivities. Courtesy, Greater Reno-Sparks Chamber of Commerce

corporate gaming laws passed the legislature in 1967 and 1969. They would have far-reaching consequences for Reno's prime growth industry—gambling, or, as the industry increasingly preferred to call itself, "the gaming industry." Reno's City Council in May of 1970 cautiously removed the old Red Line Ordinance to permit the spread of gaming establishments outside of the designated district in the downtown. It took effect January 2, 1971. Now unlimited gaming licenses would be issued only in accordance with the 100 or more hotel rooms required with each large casino and with

the general discretion of the council. Of course, new gambling applicants would also have to obtain the approval of the State Gaming Control Board.

The stage was now set for the arrival of corporate gambling investments which would cause Reno to be transformed, over the next few years, from Las Vegas' poor cousin to a town that one day might rival the colossus of the south. Older, established casinos had already begun or completed expansion plans. Harrah's built a new 24-story hotel, the Cal-Neva expanded, and Fitzgerald's added to the Reno skyline. In the 1970s new hotels and casinos such as the Sundowner, Holiday Inn, Circus Circus, Howard Johnson's in Sparks, the Reef Resort, Kings Inn, the Eldorado Hotel, and Del Webb's Sahara Reno (now the Reno Hilton) reflected the impact of corporate money on Reno gaming. In 1976 the Metro-Golden-Mayer Corporation announced its intention to build a large casino and hotel in Reno as a counterpart to its recently completed operation in Las Vegas. Its plans included a hotel of more than 1,000 rooms and one of the largest casinos in the world. The quick movement of the city to accommodate MGM and permit its construction well outside of the usual downtown gambling areas led some

A bird's eye view of the blackjack table is available through security windows that Reno casinos use to survey their customers and dealers.
Courtesy, Greater Reno-Sparks Chamber of Commerce

Below: The Reno beautification program of the 1980s hoped to convert the riverfront into a pleasant promenade with shops and restaurants. Courtesy, Greater Reno-Sparks Chamber of Commerce

Bottom: Completed in 1983, Lawlor Events Center on the University of Nevada-Reno campus offers a seating capacity of 12,000 for campus and community events. Courtesy, University of Nevada-Reno

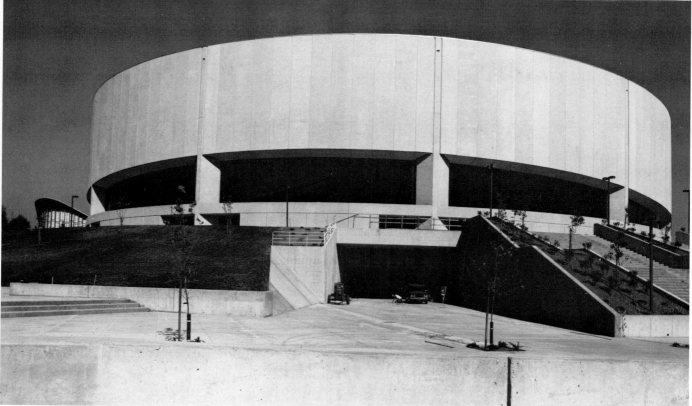

Below: Wingfield Park in busy downtown Reno offers visitors a quiet sanctuary. The spire of the historic First Methodist Church can be seen in the distance, overshadowed by high-rise casinos. Courtesy, Greater Reno-Sparks Chamber of Commerce

Bottom: The Nevada Opera Association produced the American premiere of Tchaikovsky's Joan of Arc *in the spring of 1976, translated to English by Ted and Deena Puffer. Courtesy, Nevada Opera Association*

to comment that the town had become "MGM-ized."

As the MGM tower reached skyward (the hotel opened in the summer of 1978) other corporations continued to announce their intentions to build in Reno. By the late 1970s the *San Francisco Chronicle* referred to Reno in a feature story as "Crane City" because of the numerous hotels and casinos under construction. Reno was in the midst of a crisis of growth despite the national recession of the mid-1970s. The boom in Reno led many to speculate that Reno's and Nevada's gaming economy was recession-proof. But many citizens started questioning whether the Truckee Meadows could tolerate the type of growth that some planning committees projected: a population of 388,000 was projected by the end of the century. Reno's population alone had zoomed upward from 51,470 in 1960 to 72,863 in 1970 to 100,756 in 1980. Already by August of 1978 county law-enforcement agencies reported a 20 to 35 percent increase in crime for the first half of the year and concluded, "more people means more crime."

More people also meant more demands on the resources of the Truckee Meadows, especially water. Sierra Pacific Power Company, which managed the city's water supplies, doubted the ability of the valley to sustain these growth patterns. Also the present new Reno-Sparks sewage treatment plant could not expand fast enough for the anticipated growth. Even air pollution became a problem in the valley during winter-time inversions. Added to these complications, the years from 1976 to 1979 were generally drought years, increasing doubts

about the ability of the Truckee Meadows to sustain the quality of life its people had known in the past. When proposals for the installation of water meters came from the city, many charged that the pro-growth advocates supported meters to curtail residential use so that water could be conserved for the expansion of more casinos and tourist facilities.

The growth issue suddenly became the dominant political question in Reno and Washoe County. Housing prices soared, apartments became scarce, and people were to be found on the outskirts of the city and along the Truckee camping out or living out of their cars. There might be work in Reno, but some could not afford the price of housing after

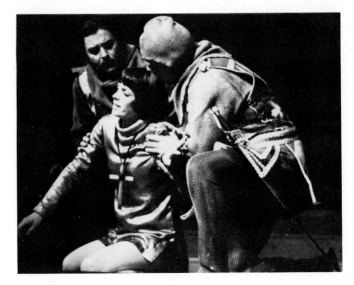

Mayor Barbara Bennett helps hold a fire hose as she and members of the Reno Jaycees launch a cleanup campaign in downtown Reno. Courtesy, Greater Reno-Sparks Chamber of Commerce

they arrived. Several casinos responded to this situation by constructing their own employee-housing facilities. With this influx Hispanics and refugees from the Southeast Asian war made their way to Reno adding to the ethnic mix in the gaming industry.

Some of the leading advocates of growth in Reno were the Chamber of Commerce under director Jud Allen and Reno mayor Bruno Menicucci. (The mayor's office was now an elected position according to a recent charter amendment, but the city-manager position remained important.) In 1979 political unknown Barbara Bennett challenged the growth policies of Mayor Menicucci running on a program of managed and studied growth. Her election victory was decisive evidence that Reno voters had become wary of some of the effects that the new prosperity brought.

Could Reno have both prosperity and a quality environment for its people? The advocates of managed growth, such as the new mayor and her supporters on the newly elected council, seemed to say yes—if the growth were managed and only the right kind of expansion allowed. But shortly after Mayor Bennett's election, the national recession of the early 1980s began to affect Reno, demonstrating that the gaming economy was not as recession-proof as its champions once proclaimed. The closure of the landmark Mapes Hotel and Money Tree Casino in 1982 was a shock to the community. The mayor and her policies came under attack for being partially responsible for the decline in the city's fortunes. When the mayor left office to assume a position with state government in the spring of 1983, many wondered if the managed-growth policies of the 1979 Council would be rejected by voters in the upcoming elections.

Former Chamber of Commerce head Allen stepped forward to run for mayor on a platform promising a return to prosperity and growth. Councilman Peter Sferrazza threw his hat into the mayoral race, indicating that he would hope to continue the managed-growth policies of mayor Bennett. In the midst of the campaign a proposal to build a vast new gaming complex on South Virginia Street across from the Centennial Coliseum came to the attention of the council. When the council returned the proposal to the Planning Commission, the project became an issue in the mayoral campaign which focused on the growth-versus-managed-growth question. In the June 1983 city elections, voters again made their decisions in favor of cautious growth by electing Sferrazza over Allen.

The Biggest Little City had come a long way from its rude beginnings as the chief waystation for the railroad in the Washoe Country, thanks partly to its people's ability to inno-

vate. Nevada's natural mineral and agricultural resources occasionally offered boom times, but these times were usually followed by the despair of borrasca and depression. In spite of the prosperity of recent years Reno's downtown stood in need of urban renewal and a general facelift. New gambling complexes sought to locate in areas other than the downtown. Along with this growing problem Reno felt keenly the need to seek more diversified industry beyond the gaming enterprises. This became particularly important with the new competition offered by Atlantic City, New Jersey. No more did Nevada have a monopoly on the industry.

In an attempt to improve the image of downtown Reno, the city embarked upon a "Renovation" campaign in the late 1960s. (Ironically, few remembered that 1930s newspaper columnist Walter Winchell had coined the term "renovation" to describe the divorce business in Reno. He suggested that people sought the "renovation" of their lives through divorce in Reno.) In the 1980s the city council launched a multi-million dollar Reno beautification program. The submitted proposals sought to take advantage of the natural beauties of the Truckee River as it flowed through town; to bring back the quiet mountain beauty that once made Reno a refuge where health, relaxation, renewal, and freedom from the cares of the world prevailed. If Reno could recapture these elements, it was felt, the city would finally be utilizing its most enduring resource and remain the hub of the Washoe Country.

From early in the century,
postcards brought greetings from
Reno to all parts of the world.

RENO IN COLOR

Beginning in 1903, the Reno Brewing Company produced a variety of beers. The One Sound State Beer emphasized a popular Nevada political slogan of the 1930s and early 1940s. The brewery sold Sierra Beer until its closure in 1957. Courtesy, Nevada Historical Society

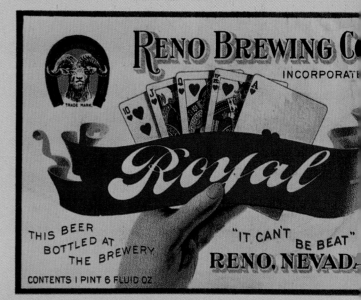

Below: Reno's Riverside Mill utilized the water power from the Truckee to mill flour sold in these colorful sacks until the Great Depression interrupted operations. Courtesy, Nevada Historical Society

Bottom: The Overland Hotel is featured in this postcard from the 1940s.

Below: Nevada News Letter offered Renoites commentaries on society, politics, business, and mining affairs from 1914 to 1927. Courtesy, Nevada Historical Society

Bottom: The cover of the sheet music to a popular song "I'm on my Way to Reno" celebrated the joys of easy divorce available in Nevada by 1910. Courtesy, University of California, Los Angeles Music Library

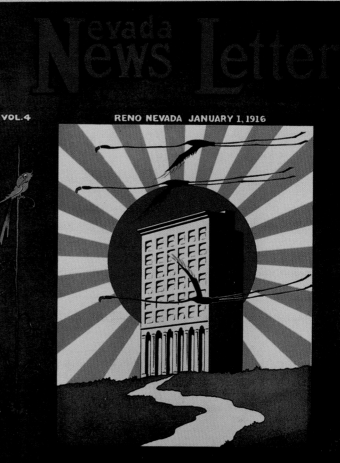

Below: Great Basin artist Jeff Nicholson depicted the plight of Paiute women in his oil painting Silent Passage. *Courtesy, Jeff Nicholson*

Bottom: From the imagination of Robert C. Caples comes The Gifts of Hy-Nan-Nu *and a legend of the Earth's beginnings. Best known for his charcoal sketches of Nevada Indian life, Caples was commissioned by Norman Biltz to do this creation in 1946. Courtesy, Nevada Historical Society*

85

Nevada artist Craig Sheppard captured the expanses of the cold desert mountain landscape along the emigrant trail near the Humboldt River in his work, West Wind. *Courtesy, Yolande Sheppard*

In the midst of the Depression Fortune *magazine carried an illustrated story on Reno titled "Passion in the Desert." The drawings by Zdzislaw Czermanski depict his view of life in a town that had become a divorce and gambling center. There is no evidence here of the chilling grip that the Depression held upon the nation. Courtesy, Nevada Historical Society*

*This pamphlet promoted Nevada's Transcontinental Highways Exposition,
held in Reno from June 25 to July 31, 1927. Presenting an exaggerated
view of the exposition grounds at Idlewild Park, the pamphlet urged
Americans to spend their vacations visiting five exhibit palaces featuring
displays of the natural resources of the Western states. Courtesy, Nevada
Historical Society*

Below: This ranch is typical of those seen in the country surrounding Reno.

Bottom: The Reno Rodeo, held in late June of each year, continues to be one of the largest and growing rodeos in the nation. Courtesy, Greater Reno-Sparks Chamber of Commerce

Below: After the death of Bill Harrah in 1978, Holiday Inns, Inc., bought his hotels and famed auto collection. Holiday Inns subsequently donated the auto collection for a museum to be built in downtown Reno as a part of the city's redevelopment plan.

Bottom: Walter Van Tilburg Clark wrote about Reno in City of Trembling Leaves. *He described Reno's tree-lined streets and quiet neighborhoods where life, romance, and death occurred untouched by the emerging "ersatz-jungle" of the city's urban center.*

Below: The Washoe County Court House became an early symbol of Reno's divorce trade as well as the seat of county government.

Bottom, left: The old McKinley Park grade school was saved from wrecking crews when it was converted into the central office of the Reno City Recreational Department in the 1970s. Photo by Susan L. Wells

Bottom, right: Typical of the statues commemorating the pioneer families of the West, this statue graces the front of Reno's Pioneer Theater Auditorium.

The steeples of St. Thomas Aquinas Cathedral have watched over the streets of downtown Reno since the church's dedication on June 20, 1908.

Visitors to St. John's Presbyterian Church are greeted by these intricately-crafted doors.

92

The Reno-Sparks Chamber of Commerce uses the slogan "Ski Reno" to promote the availability of winter sports just 45 minutes from the city. Courtesy, Greater Reno-Sparks Chamber of Commerce

Below: Since the 1920s Reno's Idlewild Park along the Truckee River has served the city's recreational needs.

Bottom: Lake Tahoe's clear blue waters offer water sports and relief from summer heat a short distance from Reno. Courtesy, Greater Reno-Sparks Chamber of Commerce

Below: The Snowbirds, the Canadian Air Force jet ace team, participated in the first Reno Air Races in 1964. Courtesy, Greater Reno-Sparks Chamber of Commerce

Bottom: Reno's night lights command the sky over the Truckee Meadows, bringing life to the city. Courtesy, Greater Reno-Sparks Chamber of Commerce

Below: At night, the streets of downtown Reno come alive with neon lights. Photo by Robert D. Stout

Below: Reno's MGM Grand Hotel features one of the largest casinos in the world. Courtesy, Greater Reno-Sparks Chamber of Commerce

Bottom: "Hello Hollywood Hello," the floor show at the MGM Grand Hotel and Casino, entertains thousands of visitors every year. Courtesy, Greater Reno-Sparks Chamber of Commerce

Reno's old and the new merge in this reflection of the Mapes Hotel in the glass exterior of the First Interstate Bank building.

CHAPTER SEVEN

PARTNERS IN PROGRESS

Reno was founded on May 9, 1868, during the construction of the Central Pacific Railroad. Formerly known as Lake's Crossing, the small developing community immediately became the supply center for the booming Comstock Lode. Its position as a rail center was improved in 1871, when the Virginia and Truckee Railroad was extended north from Carson City. Ten years later Reno became the headquarters for the narrow-gauge Nevada-California-Oregon Railroad, which served an extensive agricultural and ranching area in northeastern California and southern Oregon. Reno soon became the state's major rail center for shipping cattle and sheep to other western states.

Reno's close proximity to the lumber industry in the upper Truckee River Canyon also provided additional rail traffic and employment, as did the farms and ranches surrounding the town which produced forage crops, fruit, and vegetables in abundance.

The county seat of Washoe County was transferred from Washoe City to Reno in 1871. There were rumors of transferring the state capitol to the riverfront city. Carson City remained the capital of Nevada; however, Reno's growing population and developing business community carried much weight in state affairs.

Reno also came to occupy a dominant position in cultural and educational matters. Bishop Whitaker's School for Girls and St. Mary's Academy were excellent secondary schools that opened in the 1870s. The state legislature moved the University of Nevada from Elko to Reno in 1885. Reno also was a regular stop on theatrical circuits in the West and had several fine theaters in the community.

With the coming of the 20th-century mining boom in central and eastern Nevada, Reno became a banking and brokerage center as well as an off-loading point for supplies destined for the mining camps. The construction and settlement of the Truckee-Carson Irrigation Project, one of the nation's first federal reclamation projects, also helped Reno's economy during the first two decades of this century.

The growth of the divorce trade was another important economic development in Reno's history. In 1906 the wife of U.S. Steel Corporation president, William Corey, obtained a divorce in the city. This divorce turned Reno, with its relatively easy residency requirements, into a mecca for those seeking to dissolve their marriages. By the 1920s Reno had become the divorce capital of the world.

The completion of the transcontinental highway in the 1920s made Reno a tourist center. It was, however, the legalization of gambling in 1931 that made Reno the tourist center it is today.

The city is recognized as one of the West's most popular vacation spots. Reno is within an hour's drive of 21 major ski resorts, Lake Tahoe, historic Virginia City, and Pyramid Lake. Tourists to the area can also see the world's largest collection of antique automobiles at Harrah's Automobile Collection and one of the finest gun collections in the world at Harolds Club. In addition, visitors can find fine dining, excellent accommodations, legalized gaming, and top-name theater entertainment. In 1982 Reno was visited by over eight million tourists, who contributed heavily to the city's general economy.

In recent years Reno has become a leading distribution center of the West. The greater Reno-Sparks area's tremendous growth as an industrial and distribution center can be attributed to superior transportation facilities, excellent geographical location to western markets, an advantageous tax structure, an availability of commercial property, an abundance of power, and an adequate labor force.

In the past 115 years Reno has grown from a small river crossing to one of the fastest-growing cities in the West. The following chapter contains the histories of many local businesses that have helped to make the "Biggest Little City" what it is today. Their successes constitute an important part of Reno's history and a great source of community pride.

UNIVERSITY OF NEVADA RENO

As the University of Nevada begins its 12th decade, the institution bears little resemblance to the tiny brick building where it first opened on October 12, 1874. Elko was chosen as the site for the school because it had made the best offer to the state legislature, which had been seeking a location and funds unsuccessfully for 10 years.

For the first four years Nevada virtually had a one-man university. D.R. Sessions, a South Carolina scholar of Greek and Latin, was both

senator who had sponsored legislation for state university land-grants. Like its predecessor, the Reno school began essentially as a prep school, but by 1887 the first college-level courses were

---

Morrill Hall stands at the entrance to the historic Quad. Constructed in 1886, Morrill Hall now houses the Alumni Office, the University Foundation, and the University Press. Recently refurbished, the oldest building on the UNR campus has been placed on the National Register of Historic Places.

John W. Mackay family, who dedicated the Mackay School of Mines, one of the most prestigious branches of the university in the early 1900s. By the time of Stubbs' death in 1914, the school had produced many leading citizens of that era, and his formative influence was a major factor in its national accreditation in 1920.

The institution went through several years of political turmoil after the Stubbs administration, and World War I and the Great Depression also hampered its development. Then, under the 1938-1944 administration of Dr. Leon Hartman, the school's full-time enrollment rose to more than 1,200. In the period since World War II, this policy of expansion has continued: The university has emerged as one of the great academic institutions in the West.

the faculty and staff of the school, then called the "University Preparatory School." Unfortunately, the student body was almost as tiny as the faculty; only 20 to 30 students were served each year, and in 1885 the school was forced to move to the more populous Reno.

A site on a hill north of Reno was selected and funds were acquired for the first building, Morrill Hall, named in honor of the Vermont

introduced.

When Joseph E. Stubbs became university president in 1894, the University of Nevada began to evolve into a university in the fullest sense of the word. Distinguished faculty members were hired and respected research projects initiated; the school expanded physically to almost double its original size and it began to receive generous donations from philanthropists such as the

Today the University of Nevada Reno (UNR), one of seven institutions within the state-supported University of Nevada system, is located on 200 rolling acres north of the main business district overlooking picturesque Truckee Meadows. The campus offers baccalaureate and graduate degrees in nine major fields of study: agriculture, arts and science, business administration, education, engineering, home economics, medicine, mining, and nursing.

Noted worldwide for its high-quality faculty and progressive research programs, UNR also operates many services for the local Reno community, including continuing education, professional development workshops, a public radio station (KUNR-FM), several libraries, and the famed Fleischmann Planetarium. Celebrating its 110th birthday in 1984, UNR continues to evolve as the primary center for higher learning and career training in the state.

SHOSHONE COCA-COLA BOTTLING COMPANY

In 1935 Shoshone Coca-Cola Bottling Company was located in this building at 968 South Virginia Street. Photo courtesy of Lauren J. Ward.

The Shoshone Coca-Cola Bottling Company had its humble beginnings in a small grocery store-service station on South Virginia Street in Reno. In 1924 Leslie "Les" O. Farr, with the help of a loan from his brother, Stanley B. Farr, purchased two enterprises, the Shoshone Soda Works and the Diamond Springs Drinking Water Supply Company. During the early years the soda business accounted for just 20 percent of the profits, while the drinking water supply company brought in the other 80 percent.

About 1,600 cases of soda were sold annually. The beverages were hand bottled by Les, using a foot-operated pedal filler during free moments throughout the week at the gas station, while his 12-year-old son Curtis washed bottles on the weekends. Curtis washed 25 to 30 cases of bottles weekly. Sales were handled by young Curt Farr, who—being too young to drive—had his mother chauffeur him in the family touring car to the seven stores in the territory. Farr later joked that he was probably one of the only chauffeured salesmen in the history of the soda business.

In the 1920s Reno was the largest city in the state, boasting a population of 12,000. The trading area, due to poor roads, was limited to 400 square miles. At that time the Shoshone Soda Works marketed a wide variety of drinks, including Eagle Punch, Bluebird, and several others. This created a problem, because soda companies often changed bottle colors and styles faster than the Farrs could use up their bottles.

Business steadily improved, however, and by 1927, the year Reno celebrated the completion of the Lincoln Highway with a Transcontinental Exposition, a two-story brick building measuring 60 feet by 27 feet was constructed at 968 South Virginia Street.

The following year Stanley B. Farr officially joined the firm after he sold his Deer Park Grocery in Sparks. The main turning point in the history of the business took place in 1930, when the Coca-Cola Company of Atlanta, Georgia, awarded the Shoshone Soda Works the franchise for bottling Coca-Cola in the Reno area.

During the 1930s the market rapidly expanded, and by the end of the decade the increased demand for Coca-Cola required that additions be made in 1939 and again in 1941 to the Farrs' original plant on South Virginia Street.

Stanley Farr retired in 1957, selling all interest in the Shoshone Coca-Cola Bottling Company to his brother Les. Leslie and son Curtis operated the venture until 1970, when it was sold to Green-Hoffman Corporation, a Dallas, Texas, bottling firm. Shortly thereafter the company purchased a six-acre parcel of land near the Reno airport. A new facility was constructed at 2300 Vassar Street, and Shoshone Coca-Cola moved its entire operation there on Valentine's Day in 1972.

Under the management of Charles Leathers, the corporation has continued to expand. During the 1970s new markets were opened in eastern California, including the Quincy, Susanville, and Alturas areas. Today the Shoshone Coca-Cola Bottling Company is one of the largest Coca-Cola franchises in terms of square miles in the continental United States.

In 1938 Curtis Farr (second from left), son of the founder of Shoshone Coca-Cola Bottling Company, poses with other employees. Photo courtesy of Lauren J. Ward.

R. HERZ & BRO.

In 1897 this was the interior of the jewelry store with Richard Herz, one of the founders of R. Herz & Bro., second from left.

When Richard and Carl Otto Herz opened a small jewelry store on North Virginia Street in 1885, Reno was still a frontier town. Wagons rolled along the unpaved thoroughfare leaving ruts in the dust or mud, while pedestrians clomped along the boardwalk to pause under a druggist's mortar and pestle and a jeweler's clock for a peek into the shop. In the early days R. Herz & Bro. shared space with Pinniger's Drug Store. Once through the door, customers were greeted with the sight of a scale for weighing gold nuggets and a case full of gold-headed canes. Despite its cramped quarters the shop offered exclusive lines of watches and the finest gems and jewelry, a stock not matched by stores in many far-bigger cities. From the beginning R. Herz & Bro. gained a reputation for quality merchandise, skill in workmanship, and fair dealing.

When the Herz brothers arrived in Reno they already were experienced in the trade. Natives of Leipzig, Germany, Richard and Carl Otto began learning watchmaking and repair, engraving, and other fine points of the jeweler's art as small boys. Both worked at jewelry houses in London and New York before coming as young men to Nevada. Richard arrived in Virginia City in 1875 when the town was booming and went to work for the jewelry firm of M.M. Fredericks. Carl Otto was 22 years old when he came to the Comstock in 1884. By then Virginia

City was already on the decline, though it was still a far bigger city than Reno. Carl Otto spent a year with M.M. Fredericks before the two brothers moved to the Truckee Meadows and purchased the store owned by William Goeggel.

In the beginning the selling of diamonds and repairing of watches were the main items of business. The Herz brothers repaired their first watch shortly after opening in April 1885. By December 1889, just four years later, 3,825 watches had been repaired at the Herz store. For many years R. Herz & Bro. was the official watch repair shop for the Southern Pacific Railroad and watch inspector for the Western Pacific Railroad during its early period in Reno.

The Herz brothers soon were able to buy out the drug store and expand. The variety of merchandise expanded as well to include everything from wedding rings to grandfather clocks, to exclusive lines of the finest silverware.

In 1910 Richard and Carl Otto proposed that a gold medal be awarded to the top scholar of each graduating class at the university at the commencement proceedings. Although the school was in its 36th year as an institution and, like R. Herz & Bro., its 25th year in Reno, it had no formal way of honoring its highest achievers. In the

spring of 1910 university president Joseph W. Stubbs made the first Herz Gold Medal presentation. There was a tie for first place, however, and the Herz brothers cheerfully produced two medals for the occasion. Since then Herz medals have been awarded to 84 students.

The year 1910 was a time of mixed blessings, for the same year the Herz Medal was initiated, fire destroyed the firm's building. Richard and Carl Otto opened a new store a few doors south on Virginia Street.

Following the death of Richard in 1920, the business was operated by Carl Otto with the help of his son, Frederick. Frederick O. Herz was born in Reno. At 17 he went to Europe to travel and study. While there he mastered watchmaking and the jeweler's art. In his fourth year there World War I started and Frederick hurriedly returned to the United States, barely escaping conscription as an officer in the German Army. He continued his training with the Waltham Watch Company in Waltham, Massachusetts. When Frederick returned to Reno, he was well qualified to take his place in the jewelry firm with his father.

Upon Carl Otto's death in 1938

Ninety-eight years ago the new R. Herz & Bro. jewelry store shared this location with W. Pinniger's Drug Store. Identifiable, from left, are W. Pinniger, Richard Herz, and jewelry store clerk Willie Klippel.

Frederick became the sole owner and manager of R. Herz & Bro. In 1940 Frederick's 10-year-old son, Wilton, began working at the store with his father.

In 1942 Robert Shipley, Sr., founder of the American Gem Society, visited R. Herz & Bro. From that time on Frederick became interested in the Society and the study of gemology. Herz found that "it made the jewelry business twice as interesting and was a big help not only in buying but also in selling." In 1953 he achieved the title of registered jeweler, and in 1958 he was elected to the board of directors of the American Gem Society and became a member of the board of

R. Herz & Bro.'s second store was located at 237 North Virginia Street.

After buying out W. Pinniger's Drug Store, R. Herz & Bro. expanded its store and variety of merchandise. This location was destroyed by fire in 1910, however, and the business relocated a few doors south on Virginia Street.

place alongside her father. The company now has two stores, the more traditional downtown store at 15 North Virginia Street and a smaller branch store located in the Arlington Gardens shopping center. A visit to either store is an adventure into elegance. Finely crafted pieces of jewelry, dinnerware, clocks, and delicate knickknacks are specialties. Along with the more usual items, figurines and crystal are stocked, and at Christmastime wonderfully unique items for the holiday are featured. Those in the market for gaudy jewelry will be disappointed, for subtle beauty prevails. Prices on regular stock items are comparable to those at other stores. Customer

governors of the Gemological Institute of America.

The firm moved south again in 1954 to the Masonic Building at 15 North Virginia Street. This location is close to the scenic Truckee River. The following year the river overflowed its banks, flooding much of the downtown area, but R. Herz & Bro. survived the water and later a fire in 1965.

Wilton Herz obtained a bachelor's degree in business administration from the University of Nevada

Reno, and in 1964 he completed course work at the Gemological Institute of America in Los Angeles. Like his father, Wilton received the title of registered jeweler. When Frederick Herz died in 1972, Wilton became head of the company.

The Herz family business, now 98 years old, is the oldest jewelry firm in Nevada. The tradition of dealing only with quality merchandise, skill in workmanship, and fair dealing lives on as Wilton's daughter, Holly Muran, takes her

service is a prime concern.

Richard and Carl Otto made their homes in the little frontier town of 4,000 with the belief that Reno would someday be one of the major cities in the Intermountain West. They offered the kind of quality, selection, and craftsmanship that befitted a larger place. Today R. Herz & Bro., run by three generations of the Herz family, not only has survived but has prospered as one of Nevada's most distinctive jewelry enterprises.

PEERLESS CLEANERS

One of Nevada's oldest cleaning establishments, Peerless Cleaners is owned and operated by Fred H. Bonnenfant, a first-generation American of French descent. Fred has been in the cleaning business since 1930, and at the present location, 638 Forest Avenue in Reno, since 1949.

A self-made man, Fred H. Bonnenfant was born February 19, 1907, in Sterling City, near Chico, California, the fifth child of 10 born to Joseph and Helena (Remusat) Bonnenfant. Fred's father arrived in the United States in 1905 and went to work in the Napa vineyards. The family soon moved to Sterling City, where Fred's father worked for the Diamond Match Company. By the time Fred started school the family had moved to Loyalton, California. In 1914 the family moved to Nevada, taking up residence at the corner of Alameda and 11th streets in Reno. The father worked as a sheepherder for ranchers in the Truckee Meadows until his death in 1936.

When Fred was 11 years old his parents arranged for him to work a few weeks with a hay crew on a ranch south of town. He remembers riding the Virginia and Truckee Railroad to Brown's Station near Zollezzi Lane and being left alone with the freight with instructions from the conductor to walk a few miles more to the job. By the time Fred was 12, he was working regularly to help the family. He took a job with Henry Leter's clothing store and employment agency. He would start work at 7 a.m. and leave 10 minutes before school started each day. He worked for Henry Leter for 10 years. When his hopes of taking over the business were dashed, Fred decided to look elsewhere for a means of support.

During the summer of 1930 he filled in for the Petre brothers, French Basques, who operated National Cleaners & Dyers. Leon

Peerless Cleaners, 698 Forest Street, Reno. From left to right are longtime employee Mary Elderkin, Fred H. Bonnenfant, Jr., Maxine R. Bonnenfant, and Fred H. Bonnenfant, Sr.

Petre urged Fred to go into business for himself. In 1930 Fred purchased the Blue Goose cleaners in Sparks for $1,500. The former owner promised to stay on long enough to show him the ropes, but left shortly after the sale. Fred was rescued by an experienced worker who could neither hear nor speak. The man taught him the fine points of the cleaning business, turning a potential nightmare into a resounding success story.

Fred married Maxine E. Riley, an employee of Farmers' Merchant National Bank, in 1931. Mrs. Bonnenfant's experience at the bank proved invaluable when she joined her husband in his business. A fire damaged their building a short time later and the Blue Goose relocated at 10th and B streets. Sparks was a railroad town and the bulk of the business came from the Southern Pacific Railroad workers, particularly the conductors, who often needed their uniforms cleaned and pressed.

In 1937 Fred decided to move his business to Sierra Street, Reno, and changed the name to Lustrlux Cleaners, after one of the machine trade names. After fighting a losing battle with city parking meters installed in 1945, he moved the operation to the site on Forest Avenue in 1948. The following year the newly renamed Peerless Cleaners was hailed as one of the finest and most modern cleaning establishments in the state.

Fred and Maxine Bonnenfant, now in partnership with their son, Fred Jr., have always tried to provide the best for their customers and employees. A testament to their success, Peerless Cleaners is the oldest dry cleaning establishment in Reno, and one of the oldest in the state.

HAROLDS CLUB

When Harolds Club took over the ground floor of the Chase building it set off this celebration. A year later, 1948, the club lay claim to being the world's largest casino after acquisition of the Virginia and St. Charles hotels.

Harolds Club—Reno or Bust! For nearly 50 years this simple message spanned the globe from Casablanca to the Antarctic. The slogan revolutionized casino advertising when it was inaugurated in the late 1930s. The exciting promise of "fun" drew tourists to Reno like a magnet and made Harolds Club famous throughout the world.

When Harold Smith founded Harolds Club in the winter of 1935, the country was in the midst of the Great Depression. He recognized the need to advertise in such a way that people, despite tough economic times, would want to spend their money in Reno. The former carnival barker, in partnership with his father Raymond "Pappy" Smith, devised a planned marketing program designed to attract large numbers of gamblers to Nevada. His roadside sign campaign focused national attention upon Reno and Harolds Club.

Soon a radio and newspaper campaign followed. The newspaper ads ran from 1946 to 1956. Based on colorful events from Nevada history, the sketches appeared every week in newspapers throughout the state.

The quaint depictions of pioneer life in the West worked to promote a wholesome image of the gaming industry and brought notoriety to Harolds Club as well. The Smiths retained the frontier theme when they opened one of the club's most famous attractions, a collection of Americana featuring one of the country's most extensive accumulations of pioneer firearms.

Other innovations shocked members of the gaming industry. Smith was the first to hire female dealers, recognizing that they would bring an air of respectability to casinos. He chartered planes for gamblers from California. Customers often enjoyed drinks on the house or had their bets doubled as Harold Smith strolled past their tables.

Following World War II, Harolds Club continued to prosper as the Smiths' farsightedness brought about a revolution in Nevada's gaming industry. Further innovations became an integral part of the business, particularly the sophisticated surveillance system known as the "eye in the sky." The system, now used by most casinos in Nevada, employs a series of overhead, one-way mirrors through which employees may observe the games for any attempts to deceive the club.

The interests of the Smith family, however, went beyond the walls of their casino. They brought world-renowned concert artists to Reno for debut performances and sponsored academic scholarships at the University of Nevada.

Harolds Club has come a long way since the early days when eight employees manned one roulette wheel, one 21 game, a craps table, and two slot machines. Today the club pays millions of dollars in jackpots. More than 1,500 employees oversee 1,500 slots and 57 table games. The Smiths' belief in the power of advertising has more than paid off.

In the early 1960s three generations of Smiths, Harold Sr., founder of Harolds Club, Raymond I. "Pappy," and Harold Jr., hone their skill with a deck of cards.

Through his innovative advertising Harold Smith, Sr., helped to build Harolds Club and Reno into the gambling mecca it is today. Here he keeps his hand in at one of the gaming tables.

VALLEY BANK OF NEVADA

In 1964, when Robert Sullivan started the Valley Bank in Reno, amounts in the millions were rarely discussed by the bank's staff. After all, there were only five accounts on the bank's ledgers and only seven employees to discuss them. Yet in less than 20 years the institution has become the second-largest bank in Nevada and its largest state-chartered bank—with assets of one billion dollars.

Valley opened for business in temporary offices at 275 South Virginia Street, the first bank to open in Reno since 1939. Barely a year later the bank moved into its own building, a modern three-story structure at South Virginia and Court streets. Later, the six-floor parking garage above the bank's offices was converted into the new wing of the Pioneer Hotel.

With the motto, "Big enough to serve you and small enough to know you," the bank grew steadily throughout the 1960s. Then, in 1969, perhaps the most important event in the bank's history occurred when it merged with the Bank of Las Vegas. The merger enabled the institution to establish a statewide network of 14 branches in both southern and northern Nevada.

During the 1970s, under the direction of board chairman E. Parry Thomas in Las Vegas and president Sullivan in Reno, Valley Bank of Nevada experienced phenomenal growth. By the end of the decade the bank had doubled its number of branches and vastly increased its range of services. Known from its inception for innovation in customer services, Valley was one of the first to institute telephone banking. Called "Qwik Phone 'N Pay," customers are assigned a personal identification number, which gives them telephone access to a bank computer. Funds can be transferred 24 hours a day from savings to checking, to pay certain bills, or to determine daily balances.

Today Valley Bank of Nevada is a true full-service financial institution with 863 employees and 31 branches across the state. Its large staff of experienced personnel is trained in investment strategies for both individual and commercial clients.

In many ways, the rapid progress of the Reno community can be directly traced to the sound financial support that the bank has given to the area's business and agriculture endeavors throughout the 1970s. In addition, the bank has long held to a policy of liberal home-development financing, which has spurred the successful business, industrial, and residential climate of the community.

In a very real sense, Valley Bank of Nevada has been the solid foundation upon which Reno was built—and will continue to be so in the years ahead.

In 1964 the Valley Bank of Nevada began operations in temporary quarters at 275 South Virginia Street.

CORRAO CONSTRUCTION COMPANY

Behind the formation of successful companies often lies the fierce determination of one man or woman attempting to turn vision into reality. Corrao Construction is one of these companies, and the fierce determination belongs to Lud Corrao, who founded the Reno-based firm in 1964 and molded it into one of the largest building contractors in the United States.

Born in Brooklyn in 1937, Corrao was raised in southern California, where he majored in art and architecture. After a short period of time working as an illustrator, Corrao moved on to a seemingly more self-satisfying series of blue-collar jobs as a telephone company engineer, R & D machinist, and house builder. In 1958 he married Patricia Brunzell, whose father owned the very successful Brunzell Construction Company.

Corrao seized the opportunity to learn the construction business from the bottom up—literally—by becoming a carpenter's apprentice in his father-in-law's firm. Corrao worked for Brunzell for 12 years, learning all aspects of the business first-hand. Finally, in 1970, it was time to break out on his own.

Having already moved his family

to Reno in 1960, Corrao started his venture there. Right from the start it did well, attracting contracts for hospitals, schools, colleges, wastewater and water-treatment plants, and government agency projects in Nevada throughout the early 1970s. It was in 1972, however, that Corrao Construction began to take over a field that would solidify its reputation in the building industry—hotel and casino construction. Over the past 10 years the company has either built or renovated many of Nevada's most famous hotels—Caesar's Palace, Desert Inn, Frontier Hotel, Eldorado Hotel, Sands Hotel, Harvey's Resort, Cal-Neva, Sam's Town, Sundance, the Maxim, and many others including several in Atlantic City, New Jersey.

Utilizing his extensive art background and talent, Corrao brought the design element to the firm's construction projects. Today his firm is recognized as the premier hotel and casino builder and designer in the country after virtually reshaping the face of Las Vegas.

The philosophy of Corrao

Construction has been to combine all construction services—architecture, design, engineering, building, economics, integrity, and professionalism—into one company, thereby saving the firm's clients substantial time and guaranteeing the results. This "full-service" concept has worked so well that the Baby Grand Corporation (Corrao & Associates) became one of his own clients to prove its value. After purchasing a parcel of land on the Las Vegas Strip in 1974, Baby Grand raised the financing to build its own hotel on the property. That hotel became the Maxim, today one of Vegas' most prosperous hotels, known for its design, luxurious comfort, and spirited staff.

Though an illness forced Lud Corrao to slow his usual frenetic pace in 1981, he still manages to play an active role in the business and even to find time to consult for others. He presently is involved in oil exploration projects in Oklahoma and New Mexico, gold exploration projects in Nevada, and a major shopping center soon to open in Tonopah. Determination plus hard work may not be the only formula, but in the case of Lud Corrao they have been two major ingredients.

Caesar's Palace in Las Vegas is just one of the many hotel/casino projects constructed by Carrao Construction Company.

HARRAH'S

Harrah's Reno.

When William F. Harrah opened a bingo parlor in Reno in 1937 with six employees, he had no idea it would evolve one day into the world's largest gaming company. But that is exactly what happened: By the time of Harrah's death in 1978, he had built a company employing 7,000 people—a company considered by most analysts to be the best-managed in the gaming industry.

And yet even this remarkable growth was only a beginning. Since Harrah's became a wholly owned subsidiary of Holiday Inns, Inc., in 1980, the firm has more than doubled in almost every major yardstick of capital expansion. At the time of the merger, Harrah's operated hotel-casinos in Reno and Lake Tahoe. Since then it has opened Harrah's Marina in Atlantic City, acquired full control of the Holiday Casino Center Strip in Las Vegas, and started construction on another hotel/casino in Atlantic City to open in the spring of 1984.

From $200 million in annual revenues in 1979 the company's revenues soared to $472.8 million in 1982. Its casino space has increased 108,000 square feet to its present 201,000; its hotel rooms from 875 to 2,611; and its personnel from 7,000 to 12,000.

Quantity certainly has been an important factor in Harrah's success, but the real key has been the company's commitment to *quality*—a trait that always has been a basic policy of the parent corporation, Holiday Inns, also. William Harrah was born in South Pasadena in 1911, and grew up in nearby Venice, California. After graduating from Hollywood High School, he attended UCLA, where he studied mechanical engineering. The Depression had eaten a large chunk of the Harrah family's finances and Bill was forced to go to work at his father's struggling "circle" game parlor on Venice Beach. Then a friend suggested that Bill visit Reno to check out the little city's new downtown gambling area.

On October 30, 1937, Reno had its first Harrah-owned gambling house—a bingo parlor on Center Street. It lasted only two months due to its poor location. Dismayed but not defeated, Harrah purchased another building on Commercial Row, but this one had heating problems and by October 31, 1938, he had sold it and acquired the Heart Tango Club—an almost instant success.

Harrah's fortunes began a turn for the better. In 1941 he bought the Reno Club, another bingo establishment, and in 1942, the Blackout Bar, a full-fledged casino with 20 slot machines, one craps table, and one blackjack table. The "Harrah's Era" had begun.

The Mint Club, formerly the Block N, was purchased in 1946, and that same year Harrah's Club was opened for gaming at its present location on North Virginia Street; in 1953 Harrah bought the old Bonanza Club across the alley.

The company took a major step in 1955 when it purchased the Gateway Club at Tahoe. It was a Quonset hut located just inside Nevada on the California border. It is now the flagship of Holiday Inns/Harrah's properties—one of only three hotels in the United States with both a Mobil Five-Star and the AAA Five-Diamond ratings. And it has earned the ratings for five years in a row. The greatest names in show business play in its theater-restaurant and Harrah's Tahoe boasts more games and more slot machines than any other casino.

In Reno, the Virginia Street casino was doubled in size in 1957. Six years later a new Harrah's casino and restaurant was built on the same block adjacent to the original facility. Harrah's leased the site of its present hotel property in 1966: the Golden Hotel on Center Street. After a complete remodeling and expansion, it was reopened with the 400-seat Headliner Room theater-restaurant. This property was purchased outright in 1968, and that same year construction was started on a

106

24-story, 325-room hotel over the casino and theater-restaurant. The entire project was completed without ever interrupting business downstairs, and the hotel opened in 1969.

An important part of Harrah's operations always has been Harrah's Automobile Collection, started in 1948. Today the collection is the world's finest, with more than 1,000 automobiles. Since the collection was opened to the public in 1962, more than 4.5 million visitors have seen it.

In 1982 Holiday Inns announced that it planned to turn over the most prized cars in the collection to a public foundation. To date, 100 cars and the collection's famous research library have been donated to the Harrah Automobile Foundation. Holiday Inns plans to donate 200 to 300 more. A location for a permanent museum for the foundation's cars is being selected.

Entertainment also has been an important factor in building Harrah's worldwide fame. Harrah's now operates showrooms in Reno, Lake Tahoe, and at its Atlantic City Marina Hotel/Casino. A showroom is also planned for its new property in Atlantic City. In addition, cabarets in all of Harrah's locations present name attractions.

But gaming has been the company's mainstay and Harrah's has managed to elevate its gaming operation to the best in the industry. Harrah's trains its own dealers with as much concern for friendliness and courtesy as for technique and efficiency.

Harrah's Lake Tahoe.

Bill Harrah and the first car in his impressive collection, a 1911 Maxwell.

Harrah's Reno Hotel exemplifies the company's commitment to quality. Each guest room and bath must pass a white-glove inspection, and two crews a day inspect and clean the public areas. The new 17-story, 240-room Reno hotel tower, adjacent to the original tower, opened in 1981. The tower was the final phase of Harrah's Reno expansion, which added a two-story casino area, 235-seat cabaret, six-story parking garage, and a pedestrian skyway to the Center Street casino.

The company will continue to maintain its leadership position in northern Nevada in the years ahead. With its recently expanded lodging and casino facilities, Harrah's is perfectly positioned to meet the growing opportunities created by the city's enhanced airport and convention facilities.

Harrah's has come a long way since those early bingo parlors of the 1930s and along the way the firm has contributed immeasurably to Reno's economic stability. As the gaming arm of Holiday Inns, the world's leading hotel company, Harrah's looks forward to many more years of profitable partnership with the city of its roots.

WASHOE MEDICAL CENTER

Known as Washoe County Hospital when it was built in 1904, this building stood until 1973.

Life in the early days of Nevada afforded few luxuries, particularly for those unfortunate enough to have contracted a serious illness or suffered an injury in an accident. Professional medical care was virtually nonexistent, forcing the sick and the injured to rely upon relatives and friends. A trained physician was a rarity.

An outbreak of smallpox in 1862 at Watson's Mill near Washoe City underscored the urgent need for medical facilities, and the forerunner to Washoe Medical Center was born. The promise of competent medical care, however, did not compensate for the rundown printer's shop with a leaky roof which became the treatment center. In addition, county hospitals around the country had earned the reputation as dreaded institutions from which few came out alive. Nursing, food, and housing often were scarce and totally unsuitable for the treatment of the sick and the injured. Medical historian Henry Bergstein wrote that county facilities "in most instances were makeshifts, which were hardly

fitted for human habitations, much less for hospital purposes."

When Nevada's 19th-century mining boom turned to bust, Washoe City's population declined dramatically. In the early 1870s the county hospital moved to Second Street in Reno. The new facility was not much of an improvement: In 1873 the *Nevada State Journal* called the hospital a "hog pen—and a poor one at that."

By 1890 the increased population of Washoe County demanded the construction of a larger "poor farm" and county hospital. The new structure, located on the current site, fell conveniently outside the city limits. Citizens of Reno were concerned about the fact that the hospital often took in the county's indigent. The *Reno Crescent,* a local publication, advocated a location safely removed from the townspeople who feared "paupers afflicted with loathsome diseases."

The new building was neat and clean, but its patients, or "inmates" as they were sometimes called, had to observe strict, prison-like rules. There were closely enforced curfews, inmates could not be in or on their beds with their clothes on, they often had to work for the institution, and they could not leave without permission. Private patients also were accepted at this time. They could expect to pay the grand sum of $12 per month, a rate which was eventually reduced to $6. The hospital superintendent received $140 monthly, out of which he purchased supplies and paid the salaries of hospital employees.

Although medical attention had improved since Nevada's territorial days, all major operations continued to be referred to San Francisco hospitals. This changed in 1904, when a larger facility was constructed on the same site. The new two-story brick building was called the most prominent landmark in southeastern Reno. Nevada historian Sam Davis wrote that the new hospital boasted trained nurses, X-ray equipment, a competent bacteriologist, and the other facilities required for difficult operations. Davis also commented that Reno had become the "mecca of the afflicted," and that its medical technology attracted not only Nevadans, but those from the neighboring states of Oregon, Utah, and northern California. The new facility offered the latest in medical know-how, but the cost of equipping the hospital concerned county commissioners. The structure cost $22,000 which was raised through the sale of bonds. County officials made certain stipulations, however. A boiler and heater could not exceed $140, and surgical instruments were to be purchased for less than $100.

Washoe County Hospital continued its expansion into the 1930s, when a new building was completed facing Kirman Avenue. At this time, the institution operated under a new name, Washoe General Hospital. Nevada's growing need for sophisticated medical facilities inspired improvements and the construction of additions. The latest expansion project took place in 1973, when a $21-million addition was dedicated.

Today Washoe Medical Center serves greater Washoe County, northern Nevada, and adjacent areas of California, Idaho, western Utah, and Oregon. The facility has evolved into a fully accredited institution and is affiliated with the University of Nevada Medical School. It now offers a regional infant intensive care unit, a non-invasive vascular laboratory, a regional kidney dialysis unit, a pulmonary physiology laboratory, and the region's most

comprehensive radiology department, which features a high-speed total body scanner used to obtain cross-sectional images of a patient's brain or body. The hospital provides open-heart surgery, cardiac surgery recovery, and cardiac intensive care, in addition to a complete range of diagnostic facilities. The regional rehabilitation center offers physical, occupational, speech-language, and therapeutic recreational therapy and vocational rehabilitation. Facilities include a physical therapy gym, therapy pool, and the most modern rehabilitation equipment.

One of the oldest hospitals in the state, Washoe Medical Center boasts a history of impressive change and growth. The makeshift printer's shop has evolved into a complex regional medical center.

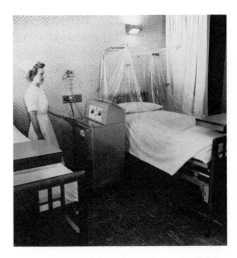

Some years back this was the newest in patient care being displayed for the opening of a new unit at Washoe Medical Center.

Today Washoe Medical Center is a fully accredited institution serving greater Washoe County, northern Nevada, and adjacent areas of California, Idaho, western Utah, and Oregon.

RENO IRON WORKS CO., INC.
Founded in 1909

Ten years ago, Reno Iron's President Andrew Ginocchio was presented with a *Builders of the Golden West Award.* Of the many awards Reno Iron Works Co., Inc., and its personnel have received, this award comes closest to capturing the essence of this company's achievements.

Ginocchio and his venture, Reno Iron Works Co., Inc., have played a significant part in almost every aspect of Nevada's building growth over the past 75 years. In 1909, the year of the company's founding, Nevada's industries were just starting to flourish. Nevada's farmers came to Ginocchio to build their newly designed wagons and farm machinery. Ginocchio also designed and produced the tools needed by the mining industry—hardrock drills and rigging tools. As mining grew throughout the state, the Reno Iron Works Co., Inc., erected buildings for these companies, many of which still stand today. During the firm's early years, the Virginia and Truckee Railroad operated trains around the clock. Keeping the V&T Railroad rolling soon became one of Andrew Ginocchio's many jobs. When the automobile came into its own, Reno Iron entered the Age of Motoring. The company built the first "Auto-Cars," which were installed on the N.C.&O. Railroad tracks running from Reno to Lakeview, Oregon.

Andrew Ginocchio (center), president, surrounded by officers of the company (left to right), Andrea Ginocchio Pelter, board chairman and controller; Bill Pelter, M.D., director; Don Jewett, vice-president; and Peg Pelter Jewett, secretary/treasurer and office manager.

This work launched diversification into truck-body manufacturing. Reno Iron Works Co., Inc., soon became a major West Coast manufacturer.

By the '20s, in response to the market's direction, the firm forged headlong into building construction. Drawing upon his earlier truck-manufacturing skills, Ginocchio built Nevada's first truck crane. From that time, Reno Iron Works Co., Inc., together with its crane fleet, fabricated and erected structural steel and miscellaneous and ornamental iron for most of

Reno Iron Works Co., Inc., is located at 600 Spice Island Drive, Sparks, Nevada.

northern Nevada's buildings, including the facilities at the University of Nevada Reno, Washoe and Douglas counties' schools, hospitals, banks, offices, hotels, and casinos. During World War II Reno Iron built most of the U.S. government installations in northern Nevada and northern California. In search of manpower for these projects, Andrew Ginocchio became a U.S. Army Corps of Engineers' instructor, certifying over 1,000 students in the period of one year. Today many leading U.S. contractors are former students of those classes held at the University of Nevada and Reno Iron's plant.

In 1937 Ginocchio became one of the major consultants on the construction of the San Francisco Golden Gate Bridge, a contribution that would lead to his *Builder of the Golden West Award.*

Today Reno Iron Works Co., Inc., with offices and the main plant located at 600 Spice Island Drive, Sparks, boasts of one of the most modern plant facilities in the United States. With 11 acres and over 91,000 square feet under roof, Reno Iron is, today, equipped with state-of-the-art robotic and computerized structural steel fabrication equipment, offering cost-effective structural fabrication and erection for a marketplace that encompasses most of the western states.

Since 1971 day-to-day operations of the company have been vested in Andrew Ginocchio's daughter, Andrea Pelter, chairman of the board and comptroller; Don Jewett, vice-president; and Peg Pelter Jewett, secretary/treasurer. However, a visitor to the plant will probably find its president, Andrew Ginocchio, at his forge, his hammer symbolically setting the tempo of Reno Iron, a tempo that will carry Reno Iron into a new era.

CLUB CAL-NEVA

Located at the corner of Second and Center streets, the gaming establishment first became the Club Cal-Neva in 1948.

The corner of Second and Center streets in Reno bustled with activity in the early evening of March 31, 1962. Anxious crowds filled the sidewalks as police units directed traffic through the area. A newcomer to Reno might have expected a parade or the arrival of a celebrity. Newspapers had heralded this gala event for days, however, and few could resist the full-page ads ringed with silver dollars.

By 6 p.m., the grand opening of the "new" Club Cal-Neva was officially under way. The patient crowd finally received their reward for waiting: Onlookers scrambled for the contents of hundreds of helium-filled balloons containing everything from silk stockings to $100 bills.

Inside, the club owners and employees worked frantically to ready the Cal-Neva for the influx of celebrants. The newspaper ads certainly paid off. Co-owner Jack Douglass recalled that there were so many people packed into the casino he could not get near the gaming area for 20 minutes. The revelers had to wait until one minute after midnight, however, before they could gamble. This was the beginning of the spring quarter under Nevada's gaming tax laws.

The Cal-Neva was not the first gaming establishment to occupy the corner of Second and Center streets. Back in the 1940s, the Club Fortune resided in a small corner of a former ladies' apparel shop. Liberace made his Reno debut there, along with the Will Masten Trio which featured a young singer named Sammy Davis, Jr. The casino was renamed the Cal-Neva in 1948, when four men from Las Vegas leased the premises. Gaming historian Raymond Sawyer notes that the new club owners were "better golfers than they were gamblers." When business began to decline in 1962, the club was sold to Leon Nightingale, Jack Douglass, Warren Nelson, Ad Tolen, Howard Ferris, and John Cavanaugh. All were experienced in the gaming industry. According to Sawyer, the six men may have represented "the most formidable array of talent in their line of work" ever assembled in Reno.

Today the Club Cal-Neva occupies a full block of downtown Reno. The owners attribute the club's success to local support. They have worked hard to promote the image of an establishment that caters to working people of the area. Double-action Keno, parlays, and 22-Ball Keno, as well as breakfast for less than a dollar, have all been successful drawing cards for the Cal-Neva. The club also was one of the first casinos to offer employee retirement and profit-sharing programs. Recently, the ownership made a million-dollar donation to the Sierra Arts Foundation.

"Good food, good service, and a fair shake" is a motto that has paid off for Reno's Club Cal-Neva.

The club now occupies a full block in downtown Reno.

FIRST INTERSTATE BANK OF NEVADA

First Interstate Bank of Nevada's head office building, Reno.

It was 1859. During the first few weeks of June, two miners poking around in the hills of western Utah Territory struck into a peculiar-looking black dirt. Further digging uncovered the upper portion of the Comstock Lode, a rich find of silver ore that would set the region on its heels.

The discovery focused worldwide attention upon the territory. Once portrayed as a barren, windswept wasteland, the Great Basin seemed less foreboding as thousands of fortune-seekers were lured to Virginia City, Queen of the Comstock.

The bonanza of bullion from its mines required the expertise of professionals trained in the handling and transportation of money. The Wells-Fargo Company was renowned throughout the West by the time it decided to extend its express services to Nevada, but its accommodations were less than fancy, comprising a tent with a sign: "Wells Fargo and Company Express." Within weeks, "and Bank" were added to the company sign, thus making it the region's first bank (of sorts).

Wells Fargo had competition, however, as other enterprising bankers set up businesses on the Comstock. Some went on to make great fortunes in banking. Others failed in the turbulent boom town atmosphere, which offered safeguards for neither banker nor depositor. It was not until 1864 that the reputable bankers of the Comstock established the protective "Nevada Bankers Association." Banking laws soon followed, but still it was an industry of chance in the true Nevada style.

This danger prompted Nevada's merchants, farmers, and business-men to establish a bank that would not be subject to the boom-and-bust nature of mining. With a backing of $100,000 and a staff of three, the Farmers and Merchants Bank opened its doors on September 17, 1902. It was Reno's "prestigious" financial institution. The bank received its national charter in 1903, thus providing a sturdy beginning for its descendant, First Interstate Bank of Nevada.

From its inception, the Farmers and Merchants Bank worked to promote an image of an institution of solidity and substance. Bank advertising was virtually unheard of until the late 1920s, when the Farmers and Merchants Bank dared to run a newspaper ad extolling the virtues of its many services. Fine marble fixtures and a spacious floor plan underscored the stability of this financial institution. The advertising campaign signaled a new era of banks actively soliciting customers.

Some of the Farmers and Merchants business practices were more straightforward and conventional, however. Vice-president Walter J. Harris' idea of security was a sawed-off shotgun in the washroom next to his desk. Without the aid of closed-circuit television, Harris nevertheless managed to communicate a tough stance against crime when he brandished his weapon.

The Farmers and Merchants Bank was renamed the First National Bank in 1929. Its solidity was put to the test two years later as banks around the country struggled to survive in the midst of the Depression.

When the financial panic of 1932 prompted Nevada's Governor Balzar to declare a bank holiday, the First National Bank in Reno refused to close. President Roosevelt called an extended bank holiday again in 1933. The President authorized a small group of banks, nationwide, to remain open. The First National Bank in Reno was among them.

By the end of 1932, only a few of Nevada's banks continued to honor their obligations to customers. The political kingpin, George Wingfield, controlled most of the state's banks. When he fell into bankruptcy, his empire fell with him and the confidence of Nevada residents in their financial institutions plummeted. Although the First National Bank was not a part of the Wingfield banking chain, it could not help but be affected by the general malaise.

Governor Balzar immediately solicited the assistance of the prestigious Transamerica Corporation of San Francisco, and a new era began in Nevada banking.

Transamerica acquired control of the First National Bank on April 20, 1934. With the collapse of the Wingfield empire, Nevada banking was in such straits that Transamerica president A.P. Giannini was handed the state of Nevada "on a silver platter," according to First National vice-president Walter Harris.

After surveying the situation, Giannini decided that Nevada was particularly suited to a branch banking system. By January the First National Bank had founded branch offices throughout the state. The extension of services restored the confidence of Nevadans in the First

---

Founded in 1902, the Farmers and Merchants Bank was a forerunner of today's First Interstate Bank of Nevada.

National Bank as well as in the state's economy.

Branch banking was by no means a fad. Rural Nevada as much as the suburbs of Reno and Las Vegas were the beneficiaries of this trend. Minden, Lovelock, and many other communities could now bank with Nevada's oldest financial institution. Subsequent years have seen explosive growth: From the summer of 1970 to the fall of 1971, six new offices of the First National Bank opened.

The First National Bank grew vertically as well as into the counties of Nevada. In 1963 the doors opened to FNB's new headquarters. The 16-floor Reno structure was the highest building in the state. It continues to serve as a symbol of the bank's solidity and substance, an image the bank has tried to convey over the years by means of its constant dependability.

MGM GRAND HOTEL-RENO

When the MGM Grand Hotel-Reno opened on May 3, 1978, it marked an important step in establishing Reno as a tourist and convention center of national significance.

Many guests have described the hotel as "a city within a city": It features seven restaurants, two cabaret lounges, two movie theaters, indoor and outdoor tennis courts, a 50-lane bowling facility, an outdoor swimming pool, and more than 40 shops and boutiques in the Grand Arcade. The property also sports a 452-space Camperland for recreational vehicles.

The MGM's convention facilities boast 30 meeting rooms, with over 140,000 square feet available for trade shows, exhibitions, banquets, and meetings. Besides business meetings and conventions, the center's facilities have been the site of beauty pageants, gymnastics tournaments, livestock auctions, and new-car introductions.

The MGM-Reno was built by Metro-Goldwyn-Mayer, Inc., and the glamour of the famous film studio is evident throughout the hotel. The Ziegfeld Theatre, which seats 2,000 for dinner and features America's largest stage, was constructed especially for Donn Arden's musical extravaganza, "Hello Hollywood, Hello!" The

The MGM Grand Hotel-Reno has become a Reno landmark, bringing visitors from every nation to "The Biggest Little City in the World."

hotel also houses the world's largest casino and has separate race and sports books and a poker room.

The hotel was a success right from the start. And as more and more tourist and convention groups from around the world stayed at the MGM, it soon became apparent that physical expansion would be necessary. In 1981, just three years after the opening, a new wing was added, increasing the number of available rooms and suites from

1,015 to 2,001. Along with the size of the hotel, the number of personnel has also grown—some 3,300 people are presently employed.

In May 1980 Metro-Goldwyn-Mayer, Inc., divided into the MGM Film Co. and MGM Grand Hotels, Inc. The latter company, which also owns the MGM-Las Vegas, is run by Alvin Benedict, chairman of the board and chief executive officer; Bernard J. Rothkopf, president and chief operating officer; and Barrie Brunet, vice-president (and president of MGM Grand Hotel-Reno). Directing the MGM-Reno operations along with Brunet are Albert Rapuano, executive vice-president, and Glenn Neely, senior vice-president.

With its luxurious rooms, suites, and comprehensive convention facilities—and its location just minutes from both Reno International Airport and downtown Reno—the MGM-Reno has been an important addition to the city's business community and a "grand" omen for the future.

Barrie K. Brunet, vice-president of MGM Grand Hotels, Inc., and president of the MGM Grand Hotel-Reno.

The grand ballroom in the MGM Grand Hotel-Reno can seat 3,400 for a sumptuous banquet and has also been the site of such diverse activities as livestock auctions, nationally televised gymnastics competitions, and trade shows and exhibitions.

SAINT MARY'S HOSPITAL

Most Reno residents trace the story of Saint Mary's Hospital back to 1908 when it first opened, but the real story begins more than a century ago, in the summer of 1877, when Mother Dolores O'Neill of Wilmington, Delaware, journeyed to Reno to found a Catholic girls' school.

Mother Dolores' school seemed to be a success right from the start. At the time Virginia and Carson cities were prosperous mining districts, and she was able to raise $3,800 to build Mount Saint Mary's Academy, a three-story structure on Fourth Street between Center and Lake. The daughters of many wealthy pioneer-miners were sent to the academy.

By the mid-1880s, however, the school began to have problems. The Nevada mining boom was ending and families were moving away; attendance at the school began to drop. Finally, in November 1892, the academy was forced to close.

Mother Dolores moved back east, but two of her novices, Sisters

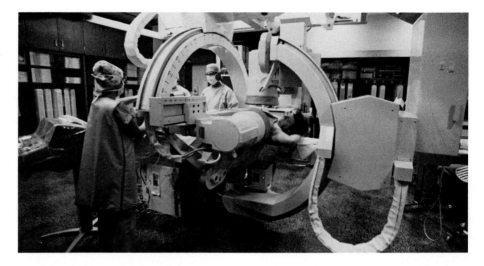

A patient undergoes examination in the new catheterization laboratory, using the bi-plane angiography unit.

In 1912 the staff of Saint Mary's Hospital poses on the steps of the newly opened building. To the right is the original school-convent, built in 1899 and converted into a hospital in 1908.

Antoine and Vincent, persevered and within a year had opened another school, this one a modest two-room schoolhouse on Sixth Street near Chestnut. The Sisters began taking in boarders and finally saved enough to construct a two-story brick building for use as a convent and novitiate in 1897.

With the turn of the century came an upswing in Reno's economic fortunes and population growth—and an accompanying need for adequate medical facilities to care for its sick. In 1908, after an epidemic of smallpox and influenza had ravaged the city, the Reno townspeople persuaded the Sisters to convert their school into a hospital. In a matter of weeks the school building was completely renovated. Saint Mary's Hospital was born.

When the Reno Sisters were accepted into the San Rafael, California, congregation, it assumed financial responsibility for the new hospital. In 1910 a nurses' training school was established at the hospital. By 1912 the hospital had become a vital part of the Reno community and a new building was constructed to replace the former schoolhouse. The 1912 building (which served as the Sisters' convent until 1980) was used as the main hospital until 1928, when the present hospital was constructed on the north side of West Sixth Street.

Since 1930 Saint Mary's has undergone numerous expansion programs to keep it one of the most modern, comprehensive health facilities in Nevada. New wings were added to the hospital in 1937, 1949, 1953, and 1965. In 1982 the new north tower addition was opened. The tower, part of a $24-million expansion project, houses the region's first full-service perinatal center and an expanded, modernized suite of surgery rooms.

Ever since Saint Mary's opened 75 years ago, the twin traditions of the hospital have been service and caring. The facility was the first in Nevada to have full-time, emergency physicians staffing its emergency department. In addition, the hospital provides medical-surgical, pediatric, and obstetrical acute care facilities; intensive care; coronary care; and an intensive care nursery.

Saint Mary's Hospital will always be ready to come to the aid of the Reno community—just as it did 75 years ago—with the finest in medical facilities, trained staff, and its long tradition of service.

LION MANUFACTURING COMPANY

The Liftall MT-80 thirty-foot forklift is just one of several varieties manufactured by Lion Manufacturing Company.

Founder Leonard Low is seen here with his wife Betty, who was an employee of the firm for many years.

There was no question that Leonard Low had a good idea. His design for a lift truck, utilizing a unique I-beam mast assembly, was so impressive that almost overnight he was able to raise $132,000 to start a company based on his truck design.

Low named his enterprise "Lion" after the venerable businessmen's club and began operating in Oakland, California, in 1965. That first year Lion Manufacturing produced 12 lifts. By 1970 output had increased to 130 trucks, and Low decided it was time for a change. He had always liked northern Nevada for its living conditions and as a plant location it had many advantages—a right-to-work state with no state income tax, a low sales tax, and an excellent business climate.

So it was that in October 1970 Lion opened a 95,000-square-foot assembly plant on Greg Street in Sparks. The Reno area has been good for the company ever since. Over the past 13 years the firm has enjoyed steady growth and momentum: From a staff of 60 in 1970 to approximately 300 in 1979, before the recession forced it to scale down for a time. It has a nationwide distribution network of more than 80 dealers and over 200 customer service and sales outlets. Its production capacity has increased dramatically; in 1979, for example, Lion manufactured 1,000 lifts in a variety of models.

With its Liftall series of forklifts, Lion is recognized as a leading manufacturer of both rough-terrain lifts and marina forklifts, designed especially for boat handling. Among producers of towable forklifts, it is ranked number one in the world. Diesel power is standard on many Liftalls and an option on most others; lift capacities range up to 80,000 pounds.

In the late 1970s Lion expanded its plant to a second building on Greg Street. Facilities now include a 24,000-square-foot product support center that handles sales, parts, shipping, transportation, and repair work.

Lion's relationship with the Reno-Sparks area has been a partnership from the beginning, just as Leonard Low thought it would be. The community has supported the company's relocation with typical hospitality and skilled labor, and the company has reciprocated with business scholarships at the University of Nevada Reno, and with several sponsorships of local sports teams.

The future holds exciting promise for Lion and its major officers: Leonard Low, chairman of the board, and his son Jim, executive vice-president. Increased emphasis on regionalization in its U.S. markets, a new product service center on the East Coast, and expansion into European and Mid-East markets are just a few of the plans that should keep Lion "king of the forklift forest" for years to come.

A partial view of Lion's machine shop and stockroom.

FIRST FEDERAL SAVINGS OF NEVADA

During Reno's early years, acquiring one's own home or business meant cash on the barrel head. Understandably, many did not have that kind of money, but a group of prominent local businessmen committed to the growth and productivity of their community wanted to change that. In 1889 a series of public meetings were held to determine the feasibility of starting a building and loan association. As a result, First Federal Savings of Nevada, then called Union Building and Loan Association, filed its articles of incorporation on April 8 of that year. It was the first organization of its kind in the state.

The company was incorporated for 5,000 shares of stock at a value of 200 par each. Stock subscriptions were taken at Folsom & Wells, the hardware store of L.D. Folsom, one of the founders and the first president of Union Building and Loan.

Union Building and Loan's office was located in Washoe County Bank on the corner of North Virginia and Second streets. In the beginning, money was sold to the highest bidder in open competition; bids ranged from 5 to 41 percent. The policy of lending money on a first mortgage secured by real estate at a reasonable rate over a given number of years was introduced by C.R. Carter, secretary under president Charles Gulling.

In 1939 the name of the organization was changed to Union Federal Savings and Loan Association of Nevada. It obtained the first federal charter in the state. In 1976, the year that the United States celebrated its bicentennial, the company changed its name to First Federal Savings and Loan Association of Nevada.

In 1989 First Federal will be celebrating 100 years of commitment

The home office of First Federal Savings of Nevada, on South Virginia Street in Reno.

to the people of Nevada. With 250 employees, the organization now has 26 offices statewide: six in Las Vegas, eight in the Reno-Sparks area, with the rest located in smaller communities around the state. Its original purpose, "to encourage development of savings habits on the part of individuals, and to supply means for families to buy or build their own homes," has become one of many goals of the present-day company. First Federal has become more than a savings and loan; it is a full-service center providing for a wide spectrum of financial needs of the community. The firm provides these services with the assistance of four subsidiaries. Eagle Service Corporation handles property

appraisals and builders' voucher control services. First Financial Service Corporation provides for property development, payroll, and word processing. TMC Financial Limited deals with real estate lending and secondary market activities, while WestMark Inc. handles marketing, research, and advertising. First Federal goes well beyond accepting deposits; it is committed to promoting both retail and wholesale savings, but also to a program that includes all types of savings plans and checking accounts, as well as retirement planning.

First Federal Savings of Nevada— like the Biggest Little City—has become more sophisticated since it was founded in 1889. Today it continues to grow and looks forward with the same pioneering spirit to its next century of service to Nevada.

PIONEER INN HOTEL/CASINO

In 1966 eight Reno businessmen—John Lazovich, Bob Lazovich, Donald J. Carano, Jerry Poncia, Bob McDonald, Tom Wilson, Frank Merrill, and Jack Lyons—formed a partnership to build a hotel-casino in Reno. United by their belief that a small hotel, with the capability of offering personalized service and a family atmosphere, would be a genuine success, they set to the task of finding the right location and financing for the project.

Two years later the Pioneer opened at 221 South Virginia Street. Designed by one of the partners, architect Jerry Poncia, the hotel had 162 rooms, a Denny's Restaurant, a lounge, and a 200-car parking lot. It was one of the last hotels built before the major corporate hotel-casino boom of the 1970s—a true pioneer that would fulfill all the founders' dreams of success.

During the first four years of the hotel's operation, the partners embarked on a steady course of expansion. In 1971 the Iron Sword Restaurant, an eatery that has evolved into a popular spot for local residents, as well as a fine dining room for guests of the hotel, was opened. That same year the Pioneer enlarged its lobby area and added 4,000 square feet of convention space, the first step in a farsighted campaign to become Reno's number-one convention facility.

The year 1974 was a landmark for the hotel: Nevada granted the Pioneer a gaming license and the hotel's casino opened with 40 slot machines and three blackjack tables. In addition, a new corporate structure was formed when Lazovich, Poncia, and Carano leased the original company from the other partners.

Throughout its history the hotel has been instrumental in attracting convention business to Reno. Working closely with the Reno Convention Bureau and other downtown hotels, the Pioneer promoted the original Fun Flights of the mid-1970s. In 1977-1978, as part

The Pioneer Inn Hotel/Casino has just been remodeled and enlarged. It now embraces an opulent Barbary Coast theme with chandeliers, mirrors, and embellishments of that era.

of another expansion phase, the hotel added more meeting rooms to its already-spacious convention facilities. Today the Pioneer can handle medium-size conventions with the most modern equipment, ample meeting and exhibit space, and the customized service that has given the hotel the reputation of being the convention headquarters of northern Nevada.

The Pioneer has always prided itself on its central location, and rightly so: In the heart of downtown Reno, it is within easy walking distance of the city's main business area, City Hall, the Washoe County Courthouse, many theaters and nightclubs, and Reno's many other casinos. Despite many expansion and remodeling programs that have increased the size of both the hotel and casino, the Pioneer has not relinquished its small-town ambience. Under the direction of managing partners Jerry Poncia and Donald J. Carano, the hotel will continue to foster the friendly atmosphere and "Pioneer spirit" that has made it a leader in Reno's tourist and business community.

JOHN HEINRICH COMPANY

"Find a need and fill it," steel magnate Henry Kaiser once advised a young entrepreneur, and John Heinrich followed Kaiser's advice to the letter when he went into business for himself in 1952. Working in Sacramento, California, at the time, he became a manufacturer's representative, developing product lines and distributing arms for California companies. In the next 30 years Heinrich must have found several needs and filled them all well, for today John Heinrich Company is a major international manufacturer of truck parts, grossing $2.5 million annually.

However, all new entrepreneurs need help, and during the formative period Heinrich was greatly assisted by Joe Fuetsch, an old friend from Firestone; Arthur Luchs of Round Chain; and George Hesik, a die-casting manufacturer.

One of Heinrich's biggest clients in the 1950s was J.C. Clark Company of Perkins, California, a truck and railroad parts manufacturer. After analyzing the firm's operations and market, Heinrich worked with Clark to add a new muffler product line and to establish a distribution system for them. Later, he introduced a new railroad tiedown to the company's line. Both product lines turned into big money-makers for Clark, and Heinrich's affiliation with the firm would play a fortuitous part in his future.

Successful consultant jobs like this made Heinrich a much-sought-after representative until 1966, when he found himself in the financial position to start his own venture. From the many companies he had worked with, Heinrich chose Bruce Wiley of Tube Craft in Cleveland, Ohio, with whom he had developed several product lines, and knew from first-hand experience that it was a solid organization with good prospects for growth.

John Heinrich, president of the John Heinrich Company.

So, the John Heinrich Company began in Carmichael, California, with a 3,000-square-foot plant. Three years later, primed for expansion, Heinrich moved the firm to a 20,000-square-foot plant in West Sacramento, where it remained until 1976. In that year, the firm moved to a 32,000-square-foot plant at 335 East Glendale Avenue in Sparks. The favorable business climate and the lower taxes, labor costs, and insurance rates have been major factors in the firm's prosperity ever since.

Today the company distributes truck exhaust and air-intake parts to an international clientele—Canada, England, Mexico, Australia, New Zealand, the Philippines, and parts of Africa. Its "Ex-Air" line of exhaust products is known nationally for both original equipment and after-market distribution and is recognized as a state-of-the-art and top-selling line west of the Mississippi. Along with the manufacturing operation, the company also maintains its long-standing manufacturers' representative business.

The enterprise has been family owned and managed for many years. John Heinrich's wife Ernestine, a former public health nurse, is treasurer and a member of the board of directors. Ernestine has played an important part in the formation and success of the company. And John Heinrich, Jr., who formerly worked for the Ford Motor Company for many years, joined the firm in 1978. L.G. Buchler of Sacramento is the secretary and rounds out the board.

The John Heinrich Company's six-year marriage with the Reno-Sparks area has been a very fruitful one, and John Heinrich expects the honeymoon to continue for years to come. For everyone concerned, that's good news for both partners.

AMERICAN SAVINGS AND LOAN ASSOCIATION

When James Lewis accepted the presidency of American Savings and Loan in 1965, Reno was experiencing some difficult times. The Air Force recently had closed down Stead Air Force Base north of Reno, business in general was on a downswing, and residents were steadily moving out of the area. Sadly, the savings and loan had been forced to foreclose on many properties and found itself holding vacant houses and apartment buildings without the realty know-how or personnel to deal with them.

A graduate of Yale University, Lewis was a senior executive for California-based Norris Industries at the time. But when an East Coast investment group purchased American and offered him the position, he accepted; the opportunity—and the challenge—were too great.

Though Lewis might have been lacking banking experience, his management and organizational skills were formidable. He immediately established a separate department to deal with the fore-closure problem. Organized along the lines of a real estate firm, the department took complete control of renting and selling the properties.

By the early 1970s American Savings had sold all the properties it had foreclosed on in the 1960s and the local economy had taken an upturn. Lewis was already deeply involved in his next major project—community development. Working with several private investors, American was able to provide financing for a number of development projects in the Reno area. The savings and loan played a crucial role in building the residential areas of Virginia Foothills, Hidden Valley, and Smithridge. The first major shopping center at Incline Village was developed on loans from American. And in the late 1970s the Eldorado, Comstock, and Onslow

The American Savings and Loan Association's first office was in this converted house shared with the realty firm of August C. Frohlich. Control of the financial institution passed to Frohlich in 1935.

Hotel-Casinos in Reno and the Golden Nugget and Maxim Hotel-Casinos in Las Vegas were financed with American loans.

The '60s and '70s saw enormous growth for the institution. The company moved its headquarters to 67 West Liberty Street in Reno, and branch offices were opened at other locations in Reno, Sparks, Incline Village, and Carson City. Three new branches were opened in Las Vegas during the 1970s, as well as the savings and loan's northernmost office in Winnemucca.

In 1977 American Savings was purchased by the Steiner Corporation, which held the company until 1982 when First Western Savings, a Las Vegas-based savings and loan with assets of $600 million, acquired it. On January 1, 1983, James Lewis became chairman of the board, and John H. Kerr, Jr., who had been instrumental in providing the valuable financial and accounting expertise during Lewis' administration, moved up from vice-president to president.

Since 1965 American's assets have grown from $15 million to $220 million. Perhaps more important, the range of services provided by the company has increased dramatically. Savings and loans are no longer mere "depositories" but rather have evolved into full-service financial centers, offering several types of checking accounts, money market instruments, and investment counseling services. As the oldest state-chartered savings and loan in Nevada, American Savings has been in the vanguard of the full-service movement, innovating many personalized services for its account holders.

Under the leadership of its creative management team, American Savings will continue to be a vital force in shaping the state of Nevada for years to come.

CARAMELLA BALLARDINI LIMITED

Today Disposal Services, Inc., serves the Reno, Sparks, and Carson City areas with this large fleet of trucks.

During the first few years of many business ventures, the founders often find themselves doing a variety of tasks. So it was when Ben Caramella and William Ceresola started the Sparks Scavenger Company, a garbage disposal service, in 1940. They not only collected their customers' trash, but also went door-to-door collecting their customers' payments.

Forty-three years later the Sparks Scavenger Company has evolved into Caramella Ballardini Limited, a wide-ranging sanitation firm serving Reno, Sparks, Carson City, indeed the entire county of Washoe. Ben Caramella still presides over the corporation, but, gratefully, he no longer goes door-to-door collecting on bills, for the company has a staff of 175 employees to handle its day-to-day operations.

Back in 1940 Caramella started Sparks Scavenger with one truck, a 1939 open-air International. The disposal charge in those days was a reasonable 50 cents per can, with a slight additional monthly charge of 25 cents for each extra can. Things went smoothly during the company's first decade—it had a contract with the city of Sparks for residential pickups—but in 1950 Caramella and Ceresola lost the contract to a rival firm.

So Caramella spent a year working on his ranch. Though it was a well-earned vacation, by 1951 he realized he needed to return to his own business. That year he founded Independent Sanitation by himself, bought his first packer truck for $13,000, and quickly acquired 200 customers.

By 1956 the company's accounts had grown to 1,000, and Caramella brought his son Jack into the business. By 1959 the firm was ready to expand to Reno. Forming a corporation with Reno businessman Larry Devincenzi, Caramella opened Reno Disposal Company with seven trucks and a small office at Sutro and East Fourth streets. Jack took over a new Carson City operation, and Caramella's other son Sam took over Independent Sanitation.

In the early 1960s the three firms went through a series of consolidations. The end result was an equal partnership among the three Caramellas, Ben's son-in-law Julius Ballardini, and Devincenzi.

Today Ben Caramella still serves the Reno, Sparks, and Carson City communities with the same orderly and efficient service that was the trademark of the original operation more than 40 years ago. As northern Nevada has grown, so has the Caramella organization. Independent Sanitation now has 8,500 accounts, Sparks has 11,000, and Reno Disposal has 23,000.

Reno's reputation for clean neighborhoods and efficient services has not come about accidentally. With the most modern refuse collection and disposal equipment available—and crews dedicated to hard work—Caramella Ballardini Limited will continue to be Reno's sanitation experts for many years to come.

Back in 1940 Sparks Scavenger Company started with one truck, this 1939 International.

PATRONS

The following individuals, companies, and organizations have made a valuable commitment to the quality of this publication. Windsor Publications and the University of Nevada Reno gratefully acknowledge their participation in *Reno: Hub of the Washoe Country.*

American Savings and Loan Association*
George and Harriet Basta
Robert and Joan Byrd
Caramella Ballardini Limited*
Centennial Plaza, Inc.
C.E.S. Screw Machine Products
City of Reno, Nevada
Club Cal-Neva*
Commercial Hardware
Corrao Construction Company*
Deluxe Travel, Owners Alan and Viive Hyman
Mead Dixon
Mr. and Mrs. Stephen H. Dollinger
Dunn/Draper/Gustin/Curtis
Fireplace Distributors of Nevada
First Federal Savings of Nevada*
First Interstate Bank of Nevada*
Edward Gera
Harolds Club*
Harrah's*
Richard and Ann Harris
John Heinrich Company*
R. Herz and Bro.*
Kelly Services, Inc.
Miriam Baron Lewis

Lion Manufacturing Company*
Joseph F. McDonald, Jr.
Dr. and Mrs. R. James Megquier
MGM Grand Hotel-Reno*
Model Dairy
Peerless Cleaners*
Dick and Charlene Pierce
Pioneer Inn Hotel/Casino*
Record Supply Co., Inc.
Reno Iron Works Co., Inc.*
John Sr. and Mildred Riggs
Saint Mary's Hospital*
Shoshone Coca-Cola Bottling Company*
Budd O. Stevenson
Stewart Title of Northern Nevada
Valley Bank of Nevada*
Washoe County Medical Society
Washoe Medical Center*
Wells Manufacturing Company
Western Nevada Supply Co.
John A. White, Jr.
White Law Chartered
William H. Whitney
Witt Properties, Inc.

*Partners in Progress of *Reno: Hub of the Washoe Country.* The histories of these companies and organizations appear in Chapter 7, beginning on page 97.

BIBLIOGRAPHY

Angel, Myron, ed. *History of Nevada.* Oakland: Thompson & West, 1881.

Bartlett, George A. *Men, Women and Conflict: An Intimate Study of Love, Marriage & Divorce.* New York: G.P. Putnam's Sons, 1931.

Boesen, Victor. *They Said It Couldn't Be Done: The Incredible Story of Bill Lear.* New York: Doubleday, 1971.

Bullis, Rose M. *History of the Washoe County Schools, 1857-1912.* Sparks: Western Printing & Publishing Company, 1977.

Clark, Walter Van Tilburg. *The City of Trembling Leaves.* New York: Random House, 1945.

_____. "Reno: The City State," in Ray B. West, Jr., *Rocky Mountain Cities.* New York: W.W. Norton, 1949.

Cline, Gloria Griffen. *Peter Skene Ogden and the Hudson's Bay Company.* Norman: University of Oklahoma Press, 1974.

Cohodas, Marvin. "Dat So La Lee and the Degikup." *Halcyon* (1982): 119-140.

Cuthrell, Faith. *Temporary Address: Reno.* New York: Farrar & Rinehart, Inc., 1941.

d'Azevedo, Warren; Don D. Fowler; Wilbur A. Davis; and Wayne Suttles. *The Current Status of Anthropological Research in the Great Basin, 1964.* Reno: Publications Division, Desert Research Institute, University of Nevada, 1964.

Deutsch, Albert. "The Sorry State of Nevada." *Colliers* CXXXV (March 18, 1955): 74-80.

Doten, Alfred. *The Journals of Alfred Doten, 1849-1903.* Walter Van Tilburg Clark, ed. 3 vols., Reno: University of Nevada Press, 1973.

Downs, James F. *The Two Worlds of the Washoe.* New York: Holt, Rinehart & Winston, 1966.

Edwards, Jerome E. *Pat McCarran: Political Boss of Nevada.* Reno: University of Nevada Press, 1982.

_____. "The Artist and Historical Reality: Walter Van Tilburg Clark and *The Ox-Bow Incident.*" *Halcyon* (1979): 77-86.

Elliott, Russell R. *History of Nevada.* Lincoln: University of Nebraska Press, 1973.

Forbes, Jack D. *The Nevada Indian Speaks.* Reno: University of Nevada Press, 1967.

Glass, Mary Ellen and Al Glass. *Touring Nevada: A Historic and Scenic Guide.* Reno: University of Nevada Press, 1983.

Glass, Mary Ellen. *Nevada's Turbulent '50s: Decade of Political and Economic Change.* Reno: University of Nevada Press, 1981.

Hamlin, John. *Whirlpool of Reno.* New York: The Dial Press, 1931.

Harrah, William F. "My Recollections of Hotel-Casino and as an Auto Collecting Enthusiast." Oral History Project, University of Nevada-Reno: 1980.

Hummel, N.A. *General History and Resources of Washoe County, Nevada.* Reno: 1888 reprint edition, Verdi, Sagebrush Press, 1969.

Hutchinson, Paul. "Nevada—A Prostitute State." *The Christian Century* XLVIII (November 25, 1931): 1488-1490.

_____. "Reno—A Wide-Open Town." *The Christian Century* XLVIII (December 2, 1931): 1519-1520.

_____. "Can Reno Be Cured?" *The Christian Century*, XLVIII (December 16, 1931): 1592-1594.

_____. "Reno's Divorce Mill." *The Christian Century* XLVIII (December 9, 1931): 1557-1559.

Leonard, Zenas. *Adventures of Zenas Leonard, Fur Trader.* John C. Ewers, ed. Norman: University of Oklahoma Press, 1959.

Lewis, Oscar. *Sagebrush Casinos: The Story of Legal Gambling in Nevada.* New York: Doubleday & Company, 1953.

Lillard, Richard G. *Desert Challenge: An Interpretation of Nevada.* New York: Alfred A. Knopf, 1942, 1949.

Mack, Effie Mona. *Nevada: A History of the State from the Earliest Times through the Civil War.* Glendale: The Arthur H. Clark Company, 1936.

Midmore, Joe. *First National Bank of Nevada.* Sparks: Western Printing and Publishing Company, 1975.

Miller, Max. *Reno.* New York: Dodd Mead, 1941.

McCarthy, Joe. "The Lincoln Highway: The First Transcontinental Paved Road." *American Heritage* XXV (June, 1974): 32-37.

Morgan, Dale L. *The Humboldt: Highroad of the West.* New York: Farrar & Rinehart, 1943.

Morgan, Neil Bowen. *Westward Tilt: The American West Today.* New York: Random House, 1963.

Norcross, F.H. "Reno: Metropolis of Nevada." *The Nevada Magazine* (August, 1899).

"Passion in the Desert." *Fortune* IX (April, 1934): 100-107.

Perry, George Sessions. "Reno." *Saturday Evening Post* CCXXV (July 5, 1952): 24-25.

Pisani, Donald J. "The Polluted Truckee: A Study in Interstate Water Quality, 1870-1934." *Nevada Historical Society Quarterly* XX (Fall, 1977): 151-166.

Prouty, Annie Estelle. "The Development of Reno in Relation to its Topography." *Nevada State Historical Society Papers* IV (1923-1924): 29-189.

Roberts, Randy. *Papa Jack: Jack Johnson and the Era of White Hopes.* New York: The Free Press, 1983.

Ronald, Ann. "Reno: Myth, Mystique, or Madness." *Halcyon* (1979): 87-101.

Rowley, William D. "In the Narrows of Nevada History." *Halcyon* (1981): 123-139.

_____. "The Truckee River." In *Rolling Rivers: An Encylopedia of American Rivers.* Richard A. Bartlett, ed. New York: McGraw-Hill, 1984.

Rusco, Elmer R. *"Good Time Coming?" Black Nevadans in the Nineteenth Century.* Westport, CT: Greenwood Press, 1975.

Sanchez, Thomas. *Rabbit Boss.* New York: Knopf, 1973.

Sanford, John. "Printer's Ink in My Blood." Reno: Oral History Project, University of Nevada, 1972.

Sawyer, Raymond I. *Reno, Where the Gamblers Go.* Reno: Sawston Publishing Company, 1976.

Schrader, Larry. *Reno Round the Clock: The True Story of America's Gambling Mecca.* New York: Exposition Press, 1954.

Scrugham, James G. *Nevada: A Narrative of the Conquest of a Frontier Land.* 3 vols., Chicago, The American Historical Society, 1935.

Shepperson, Wilbur S. *Restless Strangers: Nevada's Immigrants and Their Interpreters.* Reno: University of Nevada Press, 1970.

Skolnick, Jerome H. *House of Cards: The Legalization and Control of Casino Gambling.* Boston: Little, Brown and Co., 1978.

Smith, Harold S. *I Want to Quit Winners.* Englewood Cliffs, NJ: Prentice-Hall, 1961.

Stewart, George R. *Ordeal by Hunger: The Story of the Donner Party.* Boston: Houghton Mifflin, 1960.

Thornton, Clarence J. "C.J. Thornton, Entrepreneur, Agriculture, Business, Politics." Reno: Oral History Project, University of Nevada, 1983.

Toll, David W. *The Compleat Nevada Traveler.* Goldhill Publishing Co., 1981.

Townley, John M. *Alfalfa Country: Nevada Land, Water & Politics in the 19th Century.* Reno: Agricultural Experiment Station, Max C. Fleischmann College of Agriculture, 1981.

Turner, Wallace. *Gamblers' Money: A New Force in American Life.* Boston: Houghton Mifflin, 1965.

Twain, Mark. *The Autobiography of Mark Twain.* New York: Harper, 1917, 1959.

Vanderbilt, Cornelius, Jr. *Reno.* New York: The Macaulay Company, 1929.

Walker, M.R. *A Life's Review and Notes on the Development of Medicine in Nevada From 1900-1944.* Reno: 1944.

Webster, Stella N. "The 20th Century Club of Reno." *The Nevada Magazine* (August, 1899).

Wheat, Margaret. *Survival Arts of the Primitive Paiutes.* Reno: University of Nevada Press, 1968.

INDEX

THIS BOOK WAS SET IN
TIMES ROMAN TYPE,
PRINTED ON
70-POUND ACID-FREE MEAD OFFSET ENAMEL
AND BOUND BY
WALSWORTH PUBLISHING COMPANY
HALFTONE REPRODUCTION BY ROBERTSON GRAPHICS

Reno's famed iron bridge served townsmen from 1877 until it was replaced in 1905. Courtesy, Nevada Historical Society